Humanistic—Existential Astrology

Humanistic—Existential Astrology

Astrology

Principles and Evolution

Victor Denis Purcell

Writers Club Press
San Jose New York Lincoln Shanghai

Humanistic—Existential Astrology
Principles and Evolution

Writers Club Press
an imprint of iUniverse.com, Inc.

For information address:
iUniverse.com, Inc.
5220 S 16th, Ste. 200
Lincoln, NE 68512
www.iuniverse.com

ISBN: 0-595-14665-1

Printed in the United States of America

To Roberta Rinaldi, Randy Martin and Thomas Schovitz in appreciation for their support and encouragement over the years.

Contents

.

Chapter One

History and Evolution

"Humanists perceived the individual as a unified organism made up of autonomous drives and functions which could be differentiated from one another and integrated into a functional whole greater than the sum of its parts...It was not the outer environment that was of central importance to the humanistic psychologist, but the person's inner world of perceptions, values, thoughts, beliefs, attitudes, expectations, needs, feelings and sensations." [1]

The Zodiac (Zoe for life and Diakos for Wheel) with its twelve subdivisions, corresponding signs and relationship with the planets is a universal symbol used in almost every historic period in human history.

"In the symbolism of the Zodiac one can sense the resolve to create, as in the Tarot pack, an all encompassing archetypal pattern-a kind of figurative model to secure a comprehensible definition of each and every existential possibility in the macrocosm and microcosm." [2]

1: Perry, Glenn, Ph.D.
2: Cirlot, Pg. 384

Primitive civilization was both fascinated and sometimes frightened by the events they observed in the heavens. The movement of stars and planets as well as the faces of the Moon seemed to form a pattern that affected the change of seasons.

Historically, The earliest written astrological records date back to 3000 B. C. The King of Sargon of Agade (2750 B. C.) was said to posses a work of astrology which contained forecasts of the solar eclipses of the Sun. The Babylonians (3000 BC) (more specifically the Caldrons) are generally credited with the birth of astrology. Their charts enabled them to predict the recurrence of the seasons and certain celestial events. Through this means, the planting and harvesting of crops could now more accurately be timed.

Babylonian astrology was in turn introduced to the Greeks in the early 3rd century B. C. and through the studies of Plato, Aristotle, Pythagorus and others, it came to be highly regarded as a science. It was soon embrace by the Romans. And to this day, we still use the their names for the zodiac. In turn, the Arabs spread this discipline throughout the then known world. Other variations developed in ancient India and among the inhabitants of Central America, Mesopotamia, Egypt, Judea, Persia, India, Tibet, and Northern Europe. The earliest of Egyptian astrologers (800 BC) was Petosiris, a priest, however, the most famous was Claudius Pholemy (70 BC) who wrote Tetrabilos. This historical document is what much of modern astrology is based on.

The initial form of astrology, as noted, was used primarily to predict seasonal changes and weather patterns for agricultural purposes. Eventually it broadened to include forecasts of natural disasters, war and other mundane events such as illness, birth, death and marriages. With its growing success, it was a natural progression for astrology to begin to be used to counsel human affairs. At first kings, emperors, and various heads of state where the only ones to directly benefit from astrological intervention. However, this form of astrology was still centered on interpreting and predicting mundane events.

In more recent history, very strong advocates for astrology emerged. Among them, was Carl Jung, a noted psychiatrist, who envisioned astrology as a tool for exploring the depths of the human psyche. Some of the basic psychological tenets he wrote about are parallel to principles that have been used in astrology for centuries. One cannot help but see the similarities between his writings and the fundamentals of astrology. The planets can be compared to his concept of archetypes as the universal organizing principles underlying and motivating both individual and collective psychological life. Archetypes are original patterns or models from which all things are copied. They, in essence, are prototypes.

His principle of synchronisity, which is the simultaneous occurrence of a certain psychic state with one or more external events, echoes the fundamental Hematite statement:

"As above so as below". 3

He categorized individuals into two basic types: introvert and extrovert. In astrological terms, this is referred to as the positive and negative division of the zodiac. He further divided mankind into four distinct functioning types: intuition, sensations, thinking and feeling. This division parallels astrology's use of the four elements: Fire, Earth Air and Water.

With the advent of humanistic psychology in the 1960s many astrologers began to think seriously about their clients in terms of

---

3: Hermetic Books: collection of metaphysical works beginning from the middle of the 1st century AD to the 4th century AD. Much of it concerns astrology, alchemy, magic, and represents many of the popular ideas and beliefs of that time. It is also concerned with philosophical and theological questions. There is mentioned the concept of a one transcendent God by way we may be regenerated.

growth and transformation. This initiated the movement away from the traditional, event-oriented astrology of rigid determinism. This was an approach in which individuals were perceived as victims of a chaotic and indifferent universe over which they had little or no control. People were regarded as fated recipients of cosmic forces.

Humanistic principles stress that the process of individuation or psychic wholeness was intrinsic to mankind. Self-realization is learned from self-created experiences and we are not merely the bi-product of external forces. The emphasis was now on the potential of individuals to take responsibility for their lives, their actions and to recognize their own abilities for growth and change.

Building upon this, person-center (client-center) and existential oriented therapy developed. Person-centered theory developed by Carl Rogers believed that people are driven by an innate urge to better themselves. Each person is thought of as having the capacity for self-understanding and constructive change. Shown unconditional positive regard and a deep sense of empathic understanding, individuals could advance and move forward toward maturity, growth and personal enhancement. Existential therapy focused on such themes as personal freedom, responsibility to oneself and others and the search for meaning in one's life. Individuals were encouraged to look beyond their immediate problems in an attempt to see their difficulties or challenges as part of a greater whole.

Existential philosophy stipulates that man's central or core drive is to become an authentic being, to be able to make decisions for himself which push him onward to new experiences. This is in stark contrast to remaining stagnant in old routines and situations, which hinders growth and development. The central belief of existential philosophy is that man has the freedom to choose his own destiny. The basic decision, which we all must make, is to choose between the future and face our fear of the unknown or fall back onto the past and suffer the guilt of having missed opportunities. We, in essence, are conscious beings that are capable of making choices. We are aware of our own existence, sensations, thoughts and environment. We constantly change and create an ever-evolving image of ourselves. We create our own identity and there are no set standards or static properties established which define what it is to be human.

> *Existential psychotherapy "...is concerned with patients' ways of dealing with the fundamental issues of human existence, the meaning and purpose of life, isolation, freedom and the inevitability of death. In this method of treatment, increased awareness of the self is more important than exploration of the unconscious, but many of the techniques are borrowed from brief psychoanalytic therapy."* [4]

Another major component to this philosophical approach to life in addition to the doctrine of self-determination is the concept of self-integration. It is of utmost importance that we accept all sides of ourselves, if not, we face the possibility of being taken over and controlled by that which we disown. The significance of incorporating or combining all aspects of the individual into a whole and functioning unit, with all parts working in harmony can not be over stated. Being able to make choices in our lives depends on our level of self-awareness. To shift from determinism to self-destiny requires courage, personal responsibility and, of course, knowledge of who and what we are.

As in the practice of humanistic astrology, existential psychology focuses on the relationship of the individual and the world in which he participates. We are continually involved in defining our reality. We co-exist with our surroundings; each party influences and changes the other.

As we have noted, existential philosophy views human nature as being ever on the move and in a continuous process of unfolding or

---

4: Oxford Textbook of Psychotherapy

evolution. Each of us is continually evolving and developing, we are not static or victims of our past. The main focus in life for each of us is to live in the present. Unfortunately, it is my belief that this particular tenant of existential psychology is too limited. As our natal charts reveal, the past is a very important component in our lives. Any choice, which is made in the present, I believe, is influenced by our earliest experiences. I would add that through discovering our past, we are better able to continually re-define ourselves in the present. What existential psychology does offer, especially in this regard, is the belief that we are not imprisoned by our past and that our chief motivation in life is to define for ourselves our own identity. It is not a matter of either or but it is necessary to examine both the past and present so that they may work together for our benefit.

As mentioned, existential philosophy emphasizes mankind's ability to choose his destiny. I would add to this, that some choices are made even prior to our birth, and these choices are reflected in our natal charts. Life is based on choices, but some of these choices may originate from a much higher source then our personal, conscious ego. We may not always be aware of or necessarily consciously agree with many of our decisions even if they are necessary for our evolution. As a result, they may not easily be understood or accepted. In other words we may not conscious be aware all of the time of what choices we have made or why we have made them.

Both humanistic astrology as well as existentialism agree that we have free will. We have the ability to make free and independent choices in our lives. We are able to voluntarily make decisions that are not determined by physical forces but by personal choices. However, I would emphasize, that our natal charts suggest certain parameters in which we may operate for maximum results. These parameters are symbolized by the sign on and planets in each of the twelve houses or fields of operation in our lives. We, of course, have the option of not following this outline, as it were, but by operating within these suggested boundaries we may live our potential in this life.

It is the freedom to choose that defines humanity and each person makes choices that create his identity. This self-defining process involves commitment to and responsibility for our actions. It is the individual who creates his own meaning to his life, but he must also learn to balance his personal freedom with society's pressure to conform. I would add that even with the freedom of choice, from an astrological standpoint, operating within certain parameters as suggested by our natal chart, helps us to make better choices. Second, the choices we make may not always come from a conscious place but may originate from a much higher source. We may not fully understand or agree with these choices but nevertheless we owe it to ourselves to investigate their significance.

Central to the humanistic concept whether in psychology or astrology is the importance of developing the client's self-awareness.

Incorporating the principles of humanistic psychology in astrology, Dane Rudhyar pioneered what has come to be known as person-center astrology. The client is considered someone who has potential for growth and transformation. Rudhyar stressed that the interpretation of astrological phenomenon should be geared towards enhancing the patient's personal growth and helping him to fulfill the potentials inherent in his chart. The emphasis is not on predicting events in a person's life, but rather on attempting to understand the interpretation an individual brings to these experiences. Valuing an individual's autonomy and self-responsibility become the key issue for astrologers.

An interest in humanistic oriented astrology has continued and is thriving to this day. Such gifted astrologers as: Stephen Arroyo, Robert Hand, Howard Sasportus, Liz Greene, Karen Zondag and many others have contributed to its ever-increasing popularity.

Astro-psychology can be best summarized by the following quote:

> *"Presents a complex, multi-dimensional theory of behavior that depicts the psyche as a hierarchical structure comprised of archetypes needs, cognitive structures, emergent thoughts and behaviors and corresponding events. It is also a powerful and flexible assessment device that allows the practitioner to discern the formative experiences of childhood, gain insights into the current events and target periods of future growth. Unlike traditional-event-oriented astrology, astro-therapy is not concerned with superficial trait descriptions or the prediction of future events. Rather, it is strongly used to foster empathy for the clients internal world and thereby enhance the therapist ability to usually treat psychological problems, modify or remove existing symptoms, and promote positive personal growth and fulfillment".* [5]

Essentially, astrologers' believe that the position of astronomical bodies at the exact moment of a person's birth and the subsequent movements of those bodies reflect that person's character. The individual horoscope represents one's own unique journey or hero's quest: the precise arrangement of planets, signs and houses is the map; the astrological practitioner assists the voyager in the process of self-discovery by helping him to navigate its twists and turns.

5: Ibid

Summary of Chapter One

Mesopotamia, Egypt, Judea, India, Tibet, Northern Europe all employed some type of astrology. Earliest forms, as noted, were used primarily to predict seasonal changes and weather patterns for agricultural purposes.

In more recent times, a very strong advocate on behalf of astrology emerged. He was Carl Jung, a noted psychiatrist, who proclaimed astrology a tool for exploring the depths of the human psyche. Astrology could be utilized to, in effect, study the very soul or spirit of an individual. The mental and psychological structure of a person could be mapped out. The symbolic representation of the planets in astrological lore can be compared to his concept of archetypes, which are the universal organizing principle underlying and motivating all life. They are original patterns or models from which all other things are copied. They, in essence, are prototypes.

Building upon the precepts of humanism, person-center (client-center) and existential oriented therapy developed with the primary goal of moving the patient towards autonomy, growth and maturity. When accorded unconditional positive regard and a deep sense of empathic understanding, and when their interests, values, and dignity were respected, patients advanced.

Utilizing the principles of humanistic psychology, Dane Rudhyar pioneered what has come to be known as person-center astrology. Rudhyar stressed that the interpretation of astrological phenomenon should enhance personal growth and help implement potentials inherent in the individual's chart. The focus is not on predicting events, but on endeavoring to understand the interpretation an individual brings to his experiences. Valuing an individual's autonomy and self-responsibility, became key issues for the astrologer.

It can be stated categorically, that the what, where and how of human motivation and behavior can be deciphered on an individual by individual basis through the science and art of astrology.

Chapter Two

Vital Energy

"The Tao is the one, from the one, Yin and Yang; from these two-creativity; from energy, ten thousand things; the form of all creation to All life embodies the Yin and embraces Yang. Through their union achieving harmony" (from the Tao Te Ching)

All life is energy and is animated by an intelligent force in the universe. It is the power that governs complex processes involved in health and disease: it is the very force that animates all of life.

Historically, this vital force has been called by many different names including: Chi, (Chinese); prana (India); Ki (Japan), Whilheim Reich's Oragone; Carl Jung's Libido; Homeopathy's vital energy or simple substance.

"The vital force is an influence which directs all aspects of life in the organism. It adapts to environmental influences, it animates the emotional life of the individual, it provides thought and creatively, and it conducts spiritual inspiration....this vital force connects the individual with the ultimate unity of the universe." [6]

6: Vithoulkas, Pg. 74.

Well respected practitioners of homeopathic medicine, Dr. Burg, Dr. Herbert A. Roberts MD, and J. T. Kent MD, described this singular energy as:

"The following theory may then be formulated. The patterns or organizations of any biological system is established by a complex electro-dynamic field which is in part determined by its atomic physio-chemical compounds and which in part determines the behavior and orientation of those components. This field is electrical in the physical sense and by its properties are entities of the biological system in a characteristic pattern and is itself-in part, a result of the existence of those entities. It determines and is determined by the component.

More than establishing patterns, it must maintain patterns in the midst of a physio-chemical flux. Therefore, it must regulate and control living things. It must be a mechanism, the outcome of whose activity is wholeness, organization and continuity." [7]

"In the healthy condition of man the spirit-like vital force, the dynamism that animates the material body, rules with unbounded sway and retains all the parts of the organism in admirable harmonious vital operation as regards both sensations and function so that our indwelling reason-gift mind can freely employ this living, healthy instrument for the higher purposes of our existence." [8]

"Characterizes it as having formative conclusions, being subject to changes, pervading the material substance without replacing it,

7: H.S. Burr, Pg. 43

8: Roberts, Pg. 34.

creating order in the body, belonging to the realm of quality rather than quantity (the realm of degrees of fineness), being adaptable, and being constructive". [9]

"All operation that is possible is due to the simple substance and by it the very universe itself is kept in order. It not only operates every material substance, but it is the cause of cooperation of all things". [10]

The vitalistic energy is a phenomenological experience. It cannot be seen directly but its existence can be validated through observing the direction it takes in living organisms. It is a self-determining principle not explained by physiochemical laws but a description of the structures of experience as they present themselves to consciousness, without recourse to theory, deduction, or assumptions made from 'science'. The vital force animates all living organisms. Material exists and is preceded by and given rise to through non-material processes. Material form is based on original ideas or archetypes. This energy is not only responsible for the maintenance of life but also for its development (concept of entelly) as for example in the process of embryonic differentiation.

Historically, there have been disagreements on how the universe operates between the two major theories, materialism and vitalism. Materialism divides everything into singular events, each separate from another. This belief is rooted in Newtonian physics. This traditional, mechanical oriented physics, depicts the universe as a vast machine, whose parts move in accordance with strict physical laws and are without purpose or will. Although limited in scope, Newtonian physics does offer a reproducible and predictable look into the mechanics underlying that part of physical phenomenon which we were unable to comprehend

---

9: Vithoulkas, Pg. 74.

10: Ibid. Pg. 72

with our physical senses alone. It is the application of the principles of pure geometry to the motion of the universe.

However, in the early part of this century, Albert Einstein's Specific and General Theories of Relativity plus the discoveries made through quantum mechanics replaced the Newtonian paradigm.

> *"His (Einstein) special theory of relativity was the realization that all measurements of time and space depend on judgments as to whether two distant events occur simultaneously. This led him to develop a theory based on two postulates: the principle of relativity, that physical laws are the same in all inertial reference systems, and the principle of the invariance of the speed of light, that the speed of light in a vacuum is a universal constant."* [11]

Einstein's theories view the universe as the amalgamation of all the separate notions of space into one simple space-continuum upon which the forces of the universe play.

> *"According to classical physics, all molecules in a solid can vibrate with the amplitude of the vibrations directly related to the temperature. All vibration frequencies should be possible and the thermal energy of the solid should be continuously convertible into electromagnetic radiation as long as energy is supplied".* [12]

> *"Although quantum mechanics describes the atom purely in terms of mathematical interpretations of observed phenomena, a rough verbal description can be given of what the atom is now thought to be like…Surrounding the nucleus is a series of stationary waves;*

11: Microsoft, Encarta Encyclopedia 99 1993-1998 Microsoft Corp. *All rights: Physics*

12: Microsoft, Encarta Encyclopedia 99 1993-1998 Microsoft Corp. *All rights: Relativity*

these waves have crests at certain points, each complete standing wave representing an orbit. The absolute square of the amplitude of the wave at any point is a measure of the probability that an electron will be found at that point at any given time. Thus, an electron can no longer be said to be at any precise point at any given time". [13]

In the mid 1980s, a further refinement in physics, referred to as the string theory, developed. This theory hopes to determine what really happens at the minutest scale of physical existence where either quantum theory or relativity falls short.

In contrast to the traditional scientific methods of inquiry, these modern discoveries in the field of physics have led to the interpretation of the universe as a web of interconnected fluctuations of energy, an understanding that matter and energy are interchangeable and interrelated on a grand scale. This Unified Theory also know as the principal of symmetry emphasizes the study of large-scale relationships of the whole of existence rather than just some of its minute and observable divisions.

Fitjof Copra in his book, the *Tao of Physics* presents his understanding of the operation of the universe in the following manner:

"Sub-atomic particles are dynamic patterns which do not exist as isolated entities but as integrated parts of an inseparable network of interactions. These interactions involve a ceaseless flow of energy manifest itself as the exchange of particles. The particular interactions gave rise to the stable structures, which builds up the material world, which again do not remain static, but oscillate in rhythmic movements. The whole universe is thus engaged in endless motions in the continual cosmic dance of energy". [14]

13: Microsoft, Encarta Encyclopedia 99 1993-1998 Microsoft Corp. All rights: Quantum
14: Fritjof Capra, Pg. 207-211

Vital energy is a bi-polar phenomenon, consisting of equal but opposing energies striving for balance or homeostasis. The goal is to reach an equal distribution of energy between the negative and positive poles while simultaneously still recognizing their inherent contrast. It is this apparent contrast which produces a state of constant tension, which in turn, produces and regulates life.

In Eastern philosophy, this bi-polarism is referred to as Yin and Yang *, the two most primal components of the universe.

"*The integration of these symbols within complex patterns of 'correspondence' reaches its highest pitch of perfection in the East, where cosmic allegories (such as the Wheel of Transformation, the Yin-Yang disk, the Shivi-Juntra, etc.) provide a most intense, graphic expression of these notions on contradiction and synthesis....(The symbol is a circle bisected by a sigmoid line). Light half represents the Yang force and the dark half denotes Yin, however each half includes an arc cut out of the middle half, to symbolize that every mode must contain within it a germ of its antitheses...It is a heliocoidal symbol, a section of the universal whirlwind which brings opposites together and engenders perpetual motion, metamorphosis and continuity in situations characterized by contradiction.*" [15]

Anything automatically implies its antithesis: all action constitutes the necessity of some form of reaction: all action contains part of the negative reaction within it. All action contains within itself; it's own opposition.

---

*: Yin which Mandarin for Moon is the passive, feminine and introverted direction of energy while Yang which is Mandarin for Sun is the active, masculine and extroverted direction of energy.

15: Cirlot, Pg. 25

Binary systems are based on the premise that every natural process is comprised of two phases or aspects that are at the root of all action. Contradictory aspects within the universe are synthesized within a system of wider scope. Nothing exists which can ever represent a complete reality, but only one half of if. Each form has its analogous or counterpart force as an example: man-woman, light-dark etc. Syntheses or wholeness of any faction of reality is the result of a joining of thesis and antithesis (i.e. its opposite.)

The manifestation of vital energy in the human organism is labeled psychic energy. It is a particular form of vital energy with a specific psychic function to fulfill. It is one continuous flow of energy uniting or linking all individuals with all the forms and activities specific to the psyche.

> *"Early religious philosophies used the words "masculine" and "feminine" to differentiate between the world of idea, the logos-knowledge that comes from the mind—and the manifestation of these ideas in the material universe. The logos (symbolized by male) formulate the idea, and the feminine principle (symbolism by female) manifests the "child", or the complete entity, into the material universe…Jung says that the masculine principle represents the principal of perfection, and that the feminine represents the principal of completeness. In order to grow as human beings, in order to get a concept of self; we need to recognize the combination of these principles within others and ourselves."* [16]

In this psychic form of the vital energy, the two poles (male and female) are represented by the conscious and unconscious segments of the psyche. The first impulse is the positive movement of the individu-

---

16: Lundsted, Pg. 35 and Pg. 36

als conscious interests outward to external objects. The goal is adjustment to the outside world, to whatever exists apart from the self. The second, unconscious, represents the process of energy regressing back into the individual. It is the inward turning or contraction of the psychic energy back into the unconscious. The direction of energy is from the outside environment to the individual.

The movement of energy is from one pole to the other then back again in countless repetition; it is the attempt of an organism to create balance or remain in a state of homeostasis.

Implicit in this process is the withdrawal of energy from the opposite position: the amount of vital energy remains constant, however, its distribution at any one point varies. It is this principal of variation which forms specific energy patterns unique to each individual. In other words, it is the unique energy patterns created by fluctuations of psychic energy, which are responsible for the creation of a unique person with specific issues, personality and various characteristics solitary unto him.

Psychic energy strives to resolve and control tension and inner conflict through movement. We witness this movement in action by observing, over time, changes in a person's character or personality.

> "Vital force is capable of three forms of action: motion, direction and balance. These manifestations of energy are an integral part of an exhibition of vital energy. Growth and development are direct motion, and in the decree of their perfection do we find the manifestations of balance". [17]

From an astrological perspective, as we will see, these three forms of action are represented by the modalities.

---

17 Roberts, Pg. 54

We witness both the existence of vital energy and its individual manifestation by observing a person's astrological chart. Each chart is a unique map outlining the various potentials and characteristics of a specific person.

Key Concepts of Chapter Two

All life is energy and is animated by an intelligent force in the universe. Historically, this force has gone by many names: Chi, the Chinese word used to describe the natural energy of the universe, prana (India), Ki (Japan), Wilhelm Reich's Oragone, Carl Jung's libido, and homeopathy's vital energy or simple substance are but a few.

Vitalistic energy is a phenomenological experience. It cannot be seen directly but its existence can be validated through observing the direction it takes in living organisms. The material world exists but is given rise to through non-material processes.

In contrast, is the mechanical theory of existence, in which the universe is understood as a vast machine, whose parts move in accordance with strict physical laws that are without purpose or will. Each event or experience is separate and isolated from all others.

Vital energy is a bi-polar phenomenon comprised of negative and positive currents; they are equal but opposing energies continually striving for balance or homeostasis. They are constantly seeking or maintain internal stability, by coordinating responses of its varying factions to any and all situations that tend to disturb its normal operation. All action necessitates some form of reaction: all action contains within it, its opposite.

In man, it is labeled psychic energy, a particular form of vital energy, which we utilize. It represents a continuous flow of energy between two poles, conscious and unconscious, which unites the psyche. The first direction, conscious, represents energy moving out into the environment.

The second, unconscious, represents the energy regressing back into the individual.

Implicit in this process is the withdrawal of energy from it's opposite position: the amount of psychic energy remains constant, but its distribution at any one point varies. It is this principle of variation which forms specific energy patterns unique to each individual. In other words, it is the unique energy patterns created by the fluctuations of the psychic energy, which are responsible for the creation of a singular individual with specific issues, personality, and various characteristics unique unto him.

From an astrological perspective, we witness both the existence of vital energy and its manifestation in each individual in his natal chart. In conclusion, psychic energy strives to resolve and control tension and inner conflict through its movement.

Chapter Three

Modalities

"Two opposing electrical diodes, (positive and negative) plus the movement of the vital energy between these two poles are the three basic factors, which form the foundation of life itself. In Astrology, this phenomenon is known as the modalities".

Together they form a three-part symbol or triangle upon which the foundation of our reality is built. They are the Cardinal, Fixed and Mutable modes. From a metaphysical perspective, the triangle is a symbol of completeness; the solution to conflict posed by duality. It signifies the unification of duality into a similar experience; the triangle represents the process of reconciliation of opposing forces.

The initiating or cardinal phase represents the phenomenon in life, which is concerned with commencement or initiation towards taking some form of action. This phase is positive or the Yang side of the triangle. The fixed modality is the Yin or negative polarity of the triad. The role of this phase is to create stabilization and maturation. And finally the very moment itself of the vital energy between the two poles is adjudged the mutable mode.

This tri-part coalition represents the very cornerstone upon which all life is built: the process of action, stabilization, and finally reconfiguration.

Cardinal

This is the commencement or starting impulse of life. It is the flow of energy outward into the universe so that we may adjust to the exterior environment. The cardinal mode as it relates specifically to psychic energy represents the conscious part of the mind. It is the impetus to create, initiate and take action. Certain characteristics are associated with this style of action. People with a high percentage of cardinal in their charts may be ambitious; they are enthusiastic, have an independent nature and are able to act quickly when the circumstances call for it. The direction of the energy is outward; this allows us to adjust and interact with our surroundings.

Fixed

The fixed mode is responsible for maintaining stability. It denotes the regressive flow of psychic energy to the negative pole of the triad. It permits the unconscious part of the psyche to absorb or take in information. This mode is designated the solidifying principal of the triangle. Certain observable attributes are associated with those who have a high fixed rate in their natal charts. There is a tendency towards inertia; however this inclination also can be expressed as stability and perseverance. The person is capable of a high degree of concentration. In effect, the fixed modality creates a form of self-containment in which an individual looks within himself and not to the environment to initiate growth and change.

Mutable

The mutable triplicity symbolizes nature's continuous cycle of birth and death. Its movement is from stability to decay and destruction and finally back again to a stable configuration. This process is performed in a constant and repetitious fashion. The mutable mode represents both the progressive and regressive flow of energy from one pole to the other and then back. It is in a state of constant flux. As it was for the two preceding triplicities, certain characteristics can be observed for those with high mutable. The person is more open to change which helps them to adaptive to life's everyday fluctuating patterns.

Key Concepts of Chapter Three:

Cardinal: (The positive pole)

Cardinal energy specifically in the context of psychic energy represents the conscious part of the mind. It is the energy moving in an outward direction. It is the initiating phase representing commencement, the initial step towards taking some form of action into one's environment.

Fixed: (The negative pole)

The fixed mode represents stabilization: it is responsible for the maintenance of life in a stable form. It is the regressive flow of psychic energy toward the negative pole, or unconscious. This mode represents the solidifying principle of the triad.

Mutable: (The movement of energy between the two poles)

Mutable triplicity symbolizes the process of birth, death and the repetitions and continuous cycle of new beginnings. It is the cycle of stability, decay and destruction and finally, the start of a new periodicity.

Chapter Four

Elements

"Consciousness is primarily an organ in a world of exterior and interior experience". [18]

A major variable in the astrological lexicon is the **elements**. They are four means by which we learn who we are and about our environment. Each one of them is unique and separate from the others. They are four independent methods of learning, four ways of understanding the universe. They are the means of understanding who we are and the environment we live in.

The major goal of humanity is self-realization; through the process of learning more about ourselves, we increase our consciousness, create a set of beliefs about the world and ourselves and improve our ability to make decisions.

The four elements are *Fire, Earth, Air, and Water.* They permit us to survive in our environment.

18: Ansken

Fire inspires creativity of a spiritual kind through intuition; *Earth* helps us to adapt to environmental influences; *Air* provides thought and reflection; and *Water* animates our emotional life. Each represents four distinct methods mankind has evolved in order to function in the world of form and matter.

These four quantities are further divided into two basic divisions: active and passive: Fire and Air are active (masculine, positive) while Earth and Water are passive (feminine, negative).

The positive elements direct energy outward from the psyche into the environment. The passive elements direct energy from the environment inward into the inner world of consciousness. The later represents consuming or receiving information while the former symbolizes the utilization of that information as we interact with the environment.

They are independent methods of processing data and the primary means by which mankind interacts with the world. They involve both procuring information and interacting directly with our surroundings. We order this incoming information into categories based on their relative worth or importance to us. It is a symbiotic process: the environment helps to shape and define who we are, and in turn we alter and effect our surroundings.

The elements help us to formulate a system of beliefs about the world and ourselves. When we interact with our surroundings, we are constantly deciding what we like or dislike and what we find valuable or not. Value is what we consider as desirable, right and worth while. It is a subjective estimate of the worth, greatness, or systemic goodness of something or someone. We can assign worth and significance to objects, ideas, qualities, and abstracts concepts. Through this cataloging process we continually develop a set of beliefs about who we are based on our subjective choices. These values help provide us with a self-definition. We are exercising our free will when we make decisions regarding the worth of something we experience. As we make choices, we differentiate from others and develop a greater sense of individuality.

Through our inherent free will we are able to choose: through this process, we are constantly redefining our identity through the very decisions we make. In essence, we are what we find valuable in life.

As it was with the modalities, the elements too have their unique observable traits. An individual whose chart is comprised of mostly the positive elements (Fire and Air) is more likely to be perceived as extroverted or outgoing; he basically is oriented towards the objective or exterior world. In contrast, a person associated with the negative elements (Earth and Water) is more introverted. He is thought of as one who is more stable; his focus is on the subjective inner workings of the mind and may interpret the outer world in an even more subjective manner.

Fire

"Synthetic a priori: that which is discovered by pure intuition and is often an exact answer that the mind imposes on all objects of experience". (Kant)

Ancient Egyptian writings linked the element fire to the solar-symbolism of the flame; it was associated with the concept of life animated, with superiority and control of living matter. The alchemists of the Middle Ages considered fire the agent of transmutation because it symbolized the source from which all things are both derived from and return to; it was the agent of destruction and regeneration, a mediator between forms. In most primitive cultures, fire was connected with the Sun god, who is victorious over the force of evil. In this sense, Fire embraces both good in the sense of providing vital heat and regeneration and evil because of its destructive properties.

In ancient Greece, Aristotle proposed the existence of a world of unchanging and invisible form or ideas through which it is possible to have exact and certain knowledge. They are the ideal and perfect archetypes or original forms, and which all-material existence, is merle, a poor replica.

Fire is the faculty associated with intuition that allows us glimpses of the spiritual realm.

From the root word intueri or to look into or upon, intuition represents a type of learning involving spontaneity revelation or insight. It is the ability to extract the truth of a situation whereby it surpassing the power of the intellect alone. In a sense, it is a combination of both understanding and conviction that elevates rational knowledge to a higher level.

"Entering into the object of knowledge and knowing its essence". [19]

Essence goes beyond mere form or character of a thing. Essence represents its very heart or center. It is that part which is unique and not common to anything else. On another level, intuition can also be equated with a form of feeling response in the sense that it has a certain sensibility of comfort and rightness which allows us to accept a particular proposition. Through this faculty we are able to penetrate to the very heart of an experience. This should not be confused with the emotional component of the element water, which will be cover later.

> *"Intuition, in philosophy, (is) a form of knowledge or of cognition independent of experience or reason. The intuitive faculty and intuitive knowledge are generally regarded as inherent qualities of the mind...the concept of intuition apparently rose from two sources: the mathematical idea of an axiom (a self-evident proposition that requires no proof) and the mystical idea of revelation (truth that surpasses the power of the intellect)."* [20]

19: Bergson, Pg.7

20: Microsoft, Encarta Encyclopedia 99 1993-1998 Microsoft Corp.

This faculty for discovery is direct and spontaneous: it is the immediate apprehension of meaning behind an event, a form of cognition that is an inherent quality of the mind.

Man's intuitive abilities are a link between both the conscious mind and deep archetype structures, and the conscious mind with the external world. This process involves a complex integration of large amounts of information rather than simply gathering data. Emanuel Kant calls it a 'noumenon' or comprehension of the basic reality behind all experiences, a thing-in-itself. As the precursor of ideas, intuition affords us the ability to grasp in a holistic fashion what we perceive.

All elements have a dual function. They allow us to take in or ingest data from the environment as well as expel energy through action. Fire symbolizes our creativity. It assists us in extracting the essence of what we observe so that we may utilize our creative abilities.

Optimistic and self-confident, Fire is a risk taker, the force that blazes new frontiers. Through fire, we initiate movement and activity in the outside world. Self-assured, it is the prerequisite for adventurous activities. In mankind, it represents our quest for adventure and our faith and optimistic belief that all things are possible. In a sense, fire allows us to put a personal spin on what we experience.

Fire helps us to expand our set of values or beliefs about the world and ourselves through intuitively grasping the underlying meaning of what we experience. We then judge these experiences by our own subjective standards and subsequently place them into categorizes. We label them as intrinsically beneficial or not. It is through the subjective ordering of events in our lives that we are able to expand our consciousness. This process affords us a better understanding of our deepest motivations. We add further information and further define who we are.

The goal of Fire is to help us discover of our ultimate spiritual identity.

"It (intuition) is this type of intelligence which can be understood as the mind turning in on itself and apprehending the results of processes that have taken place outside awareness". 21

Earth

"Synthetic a posteriori: Faculty, which conveys information about the world, learned from experience, but is subject to the errors of the senses ". (Kant)

The element earth represents the world of our senses, which include hearing, sight, smell, taste and touch. This method is the most direct way of interacting with and learning about the universe. They are specialized faculties that allow us to learn about our environment in a very direct, hands on manner. It is the element most often used to orient us to the world of physical form.

Earth allows us to manage physical energy in order to secure a foundation in the world. Earth helps us manipulate raw, physical matter into useful products to insure our survival. It is sense-oriented knowledge, the product of sensory stimulus organized into comprehensive patterns. It is predicated upon the accumulation of facts and figures. A particular stimulus is received then evaluated and responded to through our specialized organs of perception. This process creates a fundamental groundwork of knowledge based upon the incoming data. Through the process of transduction into inner nerve impulses to the brain, information is instantaneously and subconsciously converted into concepts. Through this process we are able to make order out of what otherwise would seem total chaos.

21: Goldberry Pg. 137

"Earth is a symbol for direct sense experience of the physical uni-
verse, without ideas, concepts, beliefs, or wishful thinking to cloud
perception. It symbolizes the quality of being substantial and mate-
rial. It is matter and the need to deal with matter….No matter how
bound up in fantasies, idealize, or abstraction we are, we must deal
with earth and its concerns. Earth is the ultimate arena in which
the acts we perform become manifest. And in the way we usually
deal with the universe, nothing is real unless it impinges in some
way on the physical universe." [22]

Earth orients us to the world of physical form, helps us to manage energy and motivates us toward some defined and concrete goal.

Earth helps us to expand our set of values or beliefs about the world and ourselves. Through the faculty of our senses and our response to the environment, we are able to judge and subjectively categorize our experiences. As we accumulate and priorities these external stimuli, we build up a groundwork of knowledge about ourselves. We in turn estab-lish a set of values or attachments based on the principle of attraction or repulsion to external objects and events in our lives. As we priorities these external stimuli, we are able to create a set of values or attach-ments based upon our satisfaction or dissatisfaction with the outside stimuli. Through the element of earth we are able to further compre-hend who we are through our senses. Earth expands our self-under-standing. In turn we are able to further define for ourselves who we are.

Further, through earth, we learn to respect our physical limitations and develop an appreciation of our bodies and the necessity of carrying for them. Our bodies become the vessels in which the mind, feelings and intuition are united. It is through these faculties that we are able to have a direct experience with our surroundings.

22: Hand, Pg. 186

> *"We can perceive, that is to say we can ascertain the presence of something. Reliance is placed on individual observations made via the senses".* [23]

Certain traits are associated with earth: it is the world of form, self-discipline, caution, dependability, self-protection, practical reasoning and the ability to retain and act upon information. Earth is solid, reliable, practical, stubborn and possibly overly conscious but for the most part very patient and steadfast.

Air

> *"Analytical a priori: that which is exact and certain but uninformative because it makes clear only what is contained in division".* (Kant)

Air is the expression of vital energy on the cognitive plane: it is the thinking, and rational faculty. It is a system of thought that epitomizes reason in obtaining knowledge. It denotes conscious mental ability, issues involving social processes including reasoning, calculation, classifying, and intellectual oriented learning. It is the use of symbols associated with language, writing and mathematics. Air represents the predominant means of communication whether through spoken or written language.

It is an acute observer of how diverse variables relate to one another. After we have looked upon what may seem like random units of information, we are then able to organize this data into meaningful patterns.

23: Hamaker-Zondag, Pg. 53

Through Air, we are able to intellectually understand how certain relationships exist between seemingly divergent segments of the environment.

The Air element emphasis abstract form, theories, and rational and concrete facts. It is what traditional scientific investigation is modeled upon. There are three postulates, which form the backbone to the "scientific" approach:

a). **Objectivity**-observe things as they are without pre-conceived views.

b). **Acceptability**-the degree to which observations and experimentation can be reproduced.

c). **Logical deductive reasoning-Reasoning**-from theories to account for specific experimental results or that which is based on commonly accepted facts or simple observations: deductive statement would be something like: all men are mortal, Socrates is a man, therefore Socrates is mortal.

Air is concerned with carefully defined traits and characteristics of a phenomenon. And as such it also represents what we traditionally think of as memory, the process of storing and retrieving information in the brain. The four basic types of remembering are:

1). Recollection or the reconstruction of events or facts based on partial clues, which serve as reminders.

2). Recall or remembering something from the past.

3). Recognition or identifying previously encountered material as familiar.

4). Recall or learning that which has been already learned and is therefore easier to relearn.

As with all the elements, there is a strong subjective component to Air. Certain objects are perceived then assimilated and integrated into a psychic content. These bits of information are then consolidated into mental patterns. However, the choice of objects focused on, is based on a subjective judgment of external worth and value. In other words the universe is divided into segments based on our subjective intellectual judgment of what we consider is good or bad.

Air catalogs information, weighing both its prose and cons then arranges it not only in a sequential order but also into some form of hierarchy based on what we consider valuable. As a result of this intellectual belief system, we add further to our self-understanding.

Air's capacity to communicate either through the spoken or written word facilitates inner-awareness and greater social cohesion. Internal communication between various parts of our psyche permits personal solidarity. We are able to observe ourselves in an emotionally detached manner. We are capable of reflecting upon and analyzing our behavior in a straightforward fashion.

Certain traits have been associated with Air: they are a gift for planning, organizing and an ability to observe and gathered information. Air is innovative, focused on abstract ideas and has highly developed communication skills. An individual with a high quantity of air in his chart may appear detached, objective, and quick in thought and action. Air is primarily associated with left brain activity and is highly capable of creative original thinking. Its chief capability is formulating cognitive models or patterns from seemly random bits of information.

Water

> *"The symbolism of the water signs contains three cold-blooded creatures: the crab, the scorpion, and the fish. In dreams these images are usually connected with instinctual, unconscious energies that are close in the archaic natural roots of man and very remote from the world of rational, differentiated human thought. Most of water's evaluation of life is done on an unconscious level".* [24]

Water is the primal ocean and the substance from which all life emerged. The Chinese consider water the specific domain of the dragon, a symbol of good luck. In East Indian lore, water is the pre-server of life in a multitude of forms: rain, blood and milk. Water is considered limitless and immortal; it engenders the beginning and ending to all substances on earth. However, many other cultures view water as something evil: an entity that has to be conquered. Its destructive capacity is legendary. Water acts slow but steady wearing away any material it comes in contact with.

In modern psychological terms, water is generally considered the symbol of the unconscious, feminine or Yin side of our personality. It is the storehouse of unconscious and subconscious likes and dislikes, urges and compulsions. It (water) is the mediator between life and death: the symbol of both the collective and personal unconscious. It represents the struggle of our psyche to find meaningful symbols in order to be able to communicate with our conscious mind. It is the symbol of motherhood or primal mother (Magna Mater). Because of her creative and nurturing characteristics it is personified as the symbol

---

24: Greene, Liz, Relating, An Astrological Guide to Living with Others on a Small Planet (York Beach, Maine: Samuel Weiser, 1978) Pg. 69

of childhood and fertility. Although usually depicted as a feminine figure, in Russian mythology, water is a male figure called the water grandfather.

> *"This wise master is not strong ashore, but in his own element he is supreme. He inhabits the depths of rivers, streams and ponds, preferring to be close beside a millpond. During the day he remains concealed, like an old trout or salmon, but at night he surfaces, splashing and flopping like a fish, come to drive his subaqueous cattle, sheep, and horses ashore to graze or else to perch up on the mill wheel and quietly comb his long green hair and beard".* [25]

Whether portrayed as male or female, water represents a nocturnal being who is proficient in water, a force that remains a mystery relegated to be realm of the unconscious.

Water is the very foundation of life, the force that antedates all of physical creation. It is a return to the primordial state where the indisputable states of death and annihilation combine with the reality of birth and regeneration. There is a pivotal motif of immersion, a complete surrender to whatever it possesses. It causes all structures to dissolve and returned to their fluid state. Water embodies the principle of birth and contains within its symbolism, a richness of transmutation. Water is generally considered very persistent: over time, it can dissolve any substance that it wills.

Water represents emotional security and safety based upon our earliest experiences of the family. In childhood, the ability to care and provide for others and ourselves begins in our home environment. In order to overcome our inherent sense of separation and alienation this initial

---

25: Campbell, Page 80

social unit (hopefully) fostered self-acceptance and provided us a place where the personal world of feelings were developed and a strong desire to belong and feel a part of society was instilled. Water helps us to develop empathy and compassion, qualities, which allow us to experience another person's perspective on life. This ability to understand another permits us to conform and reshape ourselves to the needs of the group.

Water also encompasses relationships of the most intimate kind. It represents intimacy and procreation. In the throws of sexual passion, we experience the duality of life and death. Sex symbolizes the most heightened sense of intimacy or union through a symbolic death and surrender of our personal sense of identity to another. This process involves submitting to another's will in order for this phenomenon to take place.

Water helps us to expand our set of values or beliefs about the world and ourselves. Through our emotional responses to the environment, we are able to judge and subjectively categorize our experiences. We label them as either pleasurable or beneficial or distasteful and detrimental. Through the element of water we are able to comprehend who we are through our emotional faculties. Water expands our consciousness and affords us a better understanding of our desires, needs and emotional makeup. By knowing what we like or dislike on an emotional level, we further define who we are and further our experience of being an individual in our own right.

Water encompasses the full spectrum of human emotion: love, hate, joy, sadness etc. A person with a high ratio of water in their chart may appear empathetic, sympathetic, and compassionate. He may have a strong desire to protect, nurture and be nurtured. Water is primarily associated with right brain activity, which emphasizes creativity and spontaneity. Water represents the development of deep intimate relationships, and learning on the feeling level through our emotional faculties.

Key Concepts of Chapter Four

The four elements are Fire, Earth, Air, and Water. The positive elements (Fire and Air) direct energy outward from the psyche into the environment. The passive elements (Earth and Water) guide energy inward, into the unconscious. The latter represents ingestion of external information while the former allows us to act upon that information through our interaction with the environment. The elements are basic ways of learning about the world through perceiving and understanding it on four different levels. They are four independent methods of both processing data and interacting with the world. Each element has its unique observable characteristics:

Fire: intuitively understands and has the ability to grasp the essence of an object or experience.

Earth: includes one's body, material form in general, and the practical ability to utilize the materials of our surroundings.

Air: mental perceptions, abstracts ideas, logic, communication. The chief function is problem solving and evaluating information or ideas rationally and logically.

Water: allows us spontaneous reaction to our environment, the focus is on emotions and the ability to pick up on minute subtleties in our environment.

Key Concepts of Fire

Fire is the element associated with intuition, that particular faculty that allows us to glimpse into the basic nature of life itself. Man's intuitive abilities are a link between the conscious mind, deep archetype structures and the external world. Fire is a mediator between forms. As the precursor of ideas, intuition affords us the ability to grasp in a holistic fashion what we catch sight of and understand its essence.

Fire symbolizes a part of us that creates and is inspired by what it experiences. Optimistic and self-confidence, fire is a risk taker, the force that blazes new frontiers. Through fire, we initiate movement and activity in the outside world. The goal of this element is to help us discover our ultimate spiritual identity.

There is a very strong subjective quality to fire. Because of this faculty, we are able to shape our experiences of the outside world through our own subjective ordering of existence. In a sense, fire allows us to put a personal spin on what we experience.

Fire represents initiative, enthusiasm, and faith in one's ability to survive: it is being able to trust in the process of life itself. Through fire, we are able to discern the essence behind what we experience. We acquire information in the form of inner images, which we grasp in an instinctive, spontaneous and holistic manner. We gather this information through flashes of insights. It is the type of perception, which functions outside of the usual conscious processes and involves the integration of large amounts of information.

Key Concepts of Earth

Earth represents the world of sense perception. It allows us to manage physical energy in order to create a secure foundation in the world. It helps us to fashion physical materials into useful implements.

This element permits us to build up a groundwork of knowledge through accumulating incoming sensory data. In essence, earth is involved with synthesizing raw unorganized sensory stimuli and transmitting or converting it into inner impulses to the brain. Because of this process, we are able to make order out of the chaos of varying, incoming stimuli.

As we priorities this data, we are able to create a set of values based upon our satisfaction or dissatisfaction with the incoming external information. This helps us to better understand who we are and form a more comprising identity for ourselves.

Earth exemplifies material form in general, and our practical ability to utilize the elements of the world. We accumulate data by means of our senses. We come to know this earthly domain through our ability to see, hear, smell, taste and touch. The emphasis with earth is on gathering facts and figures, in essence to collect details.

Key Concepts of Air

Air is the expression of vital energy on the cognitive level: it is our thinking and rational faculty. It denotes conscious mental abilities, issues involving social processes such as reasoning, calculating, classifying, and intellectually oriented learning. As such, it represents our predominant means of communication. The focus with this faculty is on abstract form, theories, ideas and rational, concrete facts. Air allows us to exchange information with others whether through spoken or written language.

We intellectually observe external stimuli then place them into some form of intellectual hierarchy. Air represents the traditional scientific method of inquiry in which all knowledge is based on experience and observation. It is concerned with carefully defined traits and characteristics of a phenomenon. Ironically, even though Air is identified with logic and rational thinking, there is a very strong subjective component to it.

Certain traits have been associated with Air: a gift for planning and organizing, an ability to observe and gather information are but a few. Air is innovative, focused on abstract ideas and has highly developed communication skills. It is associated with left brain activity and is capable of creative, original thinking. Its chief quality is its ability to construct mental patterns, and is responsible for language and calculation.

Air symbolizes mental perceptions, abstract ideas, logic, and communication. The chief function is problem solving, evaluating information or ideas rationally and logically. It allows us to take what we perceive and arrange it into some form of pattern. Air is the ability to arrange facts and ideas in a meaningful sequence or hierarchy of values.

Key Concepts of Water

Water is the primal ocean, the substance from which all life emerged. The Chinese consider water the specific domain of the dragon, a symbol of good luck in their culture. In East Indian lore, water is regarded as the preserver of life in a multitude of forms: rain, blood, and milk.

In modern psychology, water is thought of as a symbol of the unconscious, feminine or Yin side of our makeup. Water symbolizes the very basis of life that precedes all form. As the feminine principle, water symbolizes birth and transmutation.

Water represents emotional security and safety based upon our earliest experiences of the family.

In order to overcome our inherent sense of separation and alienation, Water embraces relationships of the most intimate kind. This element helps us overcome this and become part of a larger aggregate.

Water can represent intimacy and procreation. As we temporarily relinquish our personal egos in order to join with another in the act of sexual union, we experience the duality of life and death. Water encompasses all shades of human emotion: love, fear, joy, sadness, etc. This element is primarily associated with right brain activity that emphasizes creativity and spontaneity. It is responsible for spatial and not-verbal concepts.

Water involves our emotions and feeling capacity. It deals with our emotional needs and desires and helps us to discover the importance of human relationships. Water evaluates information by weighing our overall emotional response to a particular stimulus. We come to know of the world through an immediate feeling response to events, ideas and people. Water affords us spontaneous interaction with the environment.

Chapter Five

Signs

*The twelve **signs** describe the qualities of an experience: they, in essence, color how a specific dimension of experience is represented. They can be thought of as adverbs describing how the action is taking place. Each sign has certain unique attributes distinguishing it from the others. For example, a planet stationed in the sign of Libra would incorporate in its expression the characteristics of balance, tack, diplomacy and impartiality. In contrast if that same planet were in Aries, the qualities of assertion, self-willfulness and a pioneering spirit would be exemplified.*

Aries is a fire, cardinal sign. It is symbolized by a Ram and is ruled by the planet Mars.

Aries is the creative impulse, the initial spark of energy manifesting into physical or material form. It is energy on an individual basis originating from the collective or primal waters of existence.

Independent oriented, Aries is a symbol of vitality and physical energy. He desires above anything else, to be first in whatever he does.

The glyph or symbol for Aries represents a seedling forcing its way up from the soil and into the sunlight. He represents the beginning of the cycle of creation. He is the creative impulse at the very moment of inception. Aries is the materialization of the vital energy from its collective source formed into a unique and individual manifestation but which is not as yet fully focused. He initiates action and movement within our environment and is the force that animates our bodies. The expression of this energy is very intense, it expresses itself in short bursts directed outward into the environment. Aries represents the very essence of the Yang or masculine energy principal. He denotes fundication or the sexual act on a deep symbolic level: it functions as the inseminating segment of fertilization, the seed from which creative activity germinates.

As with all the signs, it too helps us to enhance self-awareness and formulate a unique identity. In this particular situation, it is learning, through intuition, our physical limitations and parameters.

Aries is a pioneer, it has little concern for what others think of it; it is this stanch individualism which gives Aries it's ability to explore. To combat his overly independent nature, Aries needs to develop the capacity to see the other person's point of view, and to take other's needs, wishes, and desires just as seriously as if they were its own.

The adventurous quality of this sign helps us explore our environment. As we experience people and objects in our surroundings other then ourselves, we begin to realize that we are separate and unique beings. It is this awareness of contrasts between us versus what is out there, which begins our initial process of individuation.

In conclusion, Aries symbolizes new beginnings. Its energy is raw with no clear direction or application. It is the force of the ego drive, willful but not stabile. It has a longing to inseminate or fundicate the material and concrete realm with energy. This sign needs to learn to adjust and accept others. It has a tendency to preserve itself at all costs. This can lead to isolation or shrinking away from confrontation and mutual accommodation with others. It may even be seen as asocial or antisocial. Aries requires a great deal of freedom and does not appreciate others making demands on it. Aries can truly be considered a pioneer, one who does not want or need others approval. It has a problem with displays of emotions except for aggression or enthusiasm. It can also be impatient, lacking stamina or stick-to-ness. It is very noble and will not compromise its ideals or act in a false or deceitful manner.

Key Words for Aries

Action, ambition, antisocial, ardor, assertive, athlete, beginnings, belligerent, changeable, combative, adventurous spirit, competitive, constructive, courage, crude, desire, disregards society's conventions, drawn to physical activity, enterprising, enthusiastic, fair, foolhardy, frank, freedom oriented, generosity, good at motivating others, hardy, high energy level, impatient, imprudence, impulses, industrious, initiative, innocent, insubordinate, jealousy, lacks perseverance, lascivious, likes risk and danger, naïve, non-practical, non-reasonable, pioneer, practical, primitive, quarrelsome, self-centered, selfish, sportsmen like, stimulating.

Key Concepts for Aries

Aries is the creative impulse, the first spark of energy manifested into physical or material form. It is the movement of energy from the collective source into a unique and individual manifestation. However, it is not, as yet, focused. Aries is a symbol of vitality, independence, and physical energy.

It denotes action and movement within the environment. The expression of Aries is intense and spontaneous. It burst forth into the world. It represents the very essence of Yang or the masculine energy principal. This element helps us to enhance our self-awareness and formulated a unique identity. Through exploring our surroundings, we come to recognize as we experience ourselves in contrast with the outside environment, that we are separate and individual beings.

Taurus *is both an earth and fixed sign. The chief faculty of learning is through the senses. It is symbolize by a bull and is ruled by the planet Venus.*

Taurus is analogous to a vessel, the physical matrix or container that gives form and shape to the vital energy. Taurus helps us to appreciate the sensual and physical pleasures of this world. This enhances our sense of belonging in it. Traditionally, it is associated with accumulating material wealth.

Taurus extracts from the environment that which is valuable. It is the faculty that begins our interaction with the material plane in an earnest and focused manner. Its goal is to help build a firm foundation to sustain and preserve us here on earth.

Through our senses, we become aware of physical form and three-dimensional space. Taurus helps us to survive but most importantly, it helps us to appreciate the sensual and physical pleasures of this world.

> *"The singleness of purpose of the Taurean stick-to-itness, springs from one source: it is need for security. Self-preservation, the first law animating all nature in some degree, is the hub of the Taurean wheel of life; the Taurean curls up and dies within himself when security, emotional or material is denied".* [27]

Taurus represents our physical existence and the inherent clash between the spiritual realm and our compulsive appetites and desires which, if not checked, can run rampant. The solution to this dilemma is sublimating this energy into concrete action or work through which both the individual and society can profit.

27: Levi, Pg. 79

The harnessing of this energy into some form of positive expression helps us to discover our sense of self-worth and in turn furthers our development as individuals. Through our interaction with the external environment, we learn, based on our subjective interpretation, what we find is pleasurable or not to us.

Traditionally, Taurus is associated with accumulating material wealth. However, this characteristic is but a metaphor for our inner search for self-value. Instead of having our existence validated through material possessions or by exercising power and control over others, we are required to find it within ourselves.

In conclusion, Taurus may be considered the container for the manifestation of energy on this material plane. Being consistent and persistent, are characteristics, which enable Taurus to fertilizer or manifest the vital energy in material form. It can be very sensual, enjoys the physical world and is happy to be a part of it. Not a social sign per say, it is more interested in enjoying the physical universe rather then engaging in social activity. Taurus utilizes energy in a very practical manner. All action taken needs to be very pragmatic or objectively oriented and completed in a slow and gradual manner.

Key Words for Taurus

Accounting, affection, careful, caring, cautious, composed, conceded, constant, constructive behavior, covetous, cultured, determinant, dogmatic, earthy and sensual, exacting, fearless, firm, gentle, humor, enduring, inert, kind, lazy, limiting, motherly, obstructed, overly-sensuous, patient, perseverance, persistent, practical, protective, reserved, self-centered, selfish, self-reliant, sensitive, slow but deliberate, stable, steadfast, steady, stubborn, sympathetic, trustworthy.

Key Concepts for Taurus

Taurus is analogous to a vessel, the physical matrix or container that gives form and shape to the vital energy. It helps us to appreciate the sensual and physical pleasures of this world, which, in turn, reinforces our sense of belonging in it. Traditionally, Taurus is often associated with accumulating material wealth. However, on a more humanistic level and because it helps us to recognize and express our inherent talents, we are able to enhance our feelings of self-worth.

Gemini is both Air and mutable, it is traditionally symbolized by a pair of twins and is ruled by Mercury.

Every sign represents a particular method of learning, with Air signs it is through the intellectual or cognitive faculty. All air signs help us to relate to and understand intellectually our surroundings. Air signs tend to be in a constant state of change. Specifically in regards to Gemini, it observes and catalogs lists of information at very rapid speeds.

It is dexterous, versatile, and curious in general about how things work. Gemini represents the ability to gather a broad spectrum of knowledge. However it's method is a shotgun approach to learning. Facts are cataloged but not analyze; they are not organized into a meaningful or logical system. Therefore conclusions about what is observed cannot be drawn because the information is superficial. Gemini is the symbol of the twin; inherent in its makeup is a clash between the intellectual and emotional sides to our nature.

> *"They (Gemini) are more matter-of-fact then sentimental......They are nearly always mentally active themselves, and are quick at repartee, being bright and energetic conversationalists, good debaters, and keen at argument. There is much mental vivacity and agility".* [28]

28: Carter Pg. 69

Gemini emphasizes left brain activity or analytical thinking. However, our intellectual and emotional components need to be aligned in a harmonious working fashion, each allowed its life and respected for the contribution it makes.

In conclusion, Gemini's ability to gather information enhances our knowledge of the world and allows us to identifying with and feel a part of our surroundings. We begin to understand that although we are individuals we are also part of something larger. Gemini emphasizes cognitive processes. It has the ability to move rapidly from place to place or object to object touching lightly but without depth. It comprehends with great speed and has a very high sense of curiosity. It is very social but in a light manner with out deep connection to others. It lacks consistency and constancy because of its tendency to change rapidly and lose interest quickly. It has a very strong intellectual drive to establish connections between itself and the environment. Gemini focuses on discovering ideas but with little bother for their practical application. It may not be aware of the deeper aspects of reality but is concerned more with what is logical or rational. It has difficulty with emotions, and is not able to experience deep feelings whether ones own or others. It has very little empathy.

Key Words for Gemini

Adaptable, agile, alert, ambivalent, amoral, amusing, articulate, capricious, changeable, clever, cold, congenital, cunning, curious, detached, dexterous, dishonest, diverse, dual, eloquent, fickle, flighty, fond of trickery, gossipy, high-strung, inconsistent, informative, knowledgeable, lack of concentration, lively, logical, loquacious, manipulating, mental exploration, mentally stimulating, mobile, nervous, purposeful quick, rational, restless, scattered, scientific, shallow, skillful, sly, social, superficial, tricky, two-face, unfeeling, unreliable, varied, verbal, verbose, versatility, witty.

Key Concepts for Gemini

Each sign represents a particular method of learning; with Air, in general; it is through the intellectual faculty. Air signs represent constant change. Gemini allows us to systematically observe our surroundings at a very rapid speed. From these observations, we are able to compile lists of information. It is the first stage of learning about our environment on the cognitive level. In conclusion, this ability to gather information and enhance our knowledge of the world permits us to understand ourselves better. This awareness or self-knowledge ultimately provides us greater self-awareness and expanded consciousness.

Cancer is both Cardinal and Water. The predominant faulty of learning is through the emotions. It is symbolized by the Crab and is ruled by the Moon.

Cancer is connected with our feelings: it is a matrix that gives shape to our unstructured flow of emotions. As the complement to Capricorn, the paternal principle, Cancer symbolizes the mother. It helps us to nurture and protect both others and ourselves. She represents the capacity for self-nurturing. On a grand scale, it is the symbol of the giving or maternal side of our Source.

Cancer installs in us a desire to feel part of something; to belong, to feel connected emotionally with our surroundings. This connection is predicated upon our initial ties to our family of origin and close community. It cannot be overstated how important it is for Cancer to feel it has a family support system both in early life and as an adult.

Cancer is very sensitive and self-protective in general, but especially when it comes to its emotions. As a cardinal sign, it can be very tenacious in controlling itself and others in order to feel emotionally secure.

Cancer helps us to become nurturing beings. It teaches us how to take in and assimilated impressions from the outer world through our feeling nature. Instead of learning about our environment on just an intellectual level, we are able to experience it very deeply through our emotions.

In conclusion, Cancer represents the complete development of the individual through the unfolding of the emotional faculties. Its focus is on feelings and being a part of something, that is having a sense of belonging. This is usually fulfilled in small groups or within the family unit. It has a very strong connection to the past especially to family, community and childhood. Cancer has an unwavering need for emotional security especially to feel nurtured through a supportive environment. It also has a strong desire to give support and to nurture. If its needs are not met, it can lash out in a childish manner. This can lead it to become overly dependent or grasping. It can be possessive and smothering in an attempt to feel secure. It is very community oriented and can offer society its nurturing capabilities.

Key Words for Cancer

A homebody, aware of feelings, caring, childish, childlike, clinging, clings to past, comfort, conscious, conservative, deeply feeling, delicate, dependent, difficult with criticism, domestic, easily hurt, emotional, emotionally insecure, empathetic, family oriented, family, fearful, feeling, focus on past, grasp, helpless, home, hypersensitive, hysterical, indulgent, innocent, intuitive, loyal, martyr-like, maternal, moody, need for emotional relationships, need to feel that one belongs, needy, nurture, overly emotional protective, overly emotional, overly impressionable, overly responsive, parasites, passive, pathetic, personable, processing, protective, psychic, receptive, reclusive, responsible, secretive, security oriented, sees self in others, self-absorbing, self-efficient, selfish, self-pity, self-protective, sensitive, shrewd, smothering, soft, supportive, sympathetic, tenacious, tendency to worry, thinskinned, thrifty, suffocating, timid, touchy, warm hearted, withdrawn for protection, withheld.

Key Concepts for Cancer

Cancer is associated with our emotions: it is a matrix that gives shape and structure to them. As the complement to Capricorn, the paternal principle, Cancer symbolizes the maternal principle. In human development, this crab phase signifies that the emotions aroused by the environment have to be assimilated and that the inner emotional component of life has to be reconciled. In conclusion, Cancer helps us to become nurturing beings.

> **Leo** *is both a fire and fixed sign. A lion symbolizes it. Its chief faculty of learning is through the intuition. It is ruled by the Sun.*

Despite the cliché that Leo is the entertainer, the truth is, this most noble of signs is highly spiritual. In its true sense, it represents a search for our spiritual origins. The Leo's need for recognition, appreciation and notoriety are symbolic of its urgent need to be recognized as a unique entity. Blatant displays of showmanship are misdirected attempts to gain recognition from external sources instead of from within. However, when all is said and done, Leos can like the spotlight.

Leo is associated with the father archetype. It is through our creative endeavors that we directly experience our connection with our Higher Source or Original Creator. Leo represents the true search for our inner self or spiritual core. Through this sign we express in material form, our inner creative urge. As we utilize these abilities, we reconnect with our spiritual roots. The goal of Leo is to develop confidence in ourselves through our creative expressions. Although there is a tendency to idealize itself and to be a bit of an exhibitionist, this distinction is but a tool to assist us in becoming more self-aware in order to discover and express ours aesthetic abilities.

The supposed notorious self-centeredness of Leo is really a misguided attempt at self-recognition, not ego recognition, but the type, which originates from our true Source.

The fundamental journey of Leo is to discover who we are and why we are here, our unique purpose in life. Through expressing our creative talents we begin to learn what we truly stand for and where we are evolving. Leo has a strong desire to develop power, authority and of course, artistic expression. The desired outcome is to emerge as an individual in our own right. In order for this to happen, we need to have a healthy sense of our own creativity, authority and worth. On the positive side, we may express this need through actualizing our abilities. The negative manifestation may be an attempt to control others, a blatant misuse of power.

Leo needs to learn to respect the needs of the larger society, the importance of one to one relationships and to appreciate the uniqueness of others.

In the Leo stage, we are learning to develop confidence, to radiate ourselves outward into the environment, to find out who we are and to express our creativity. This sign's journey is that of the hero, one who mythologies life, one who idealize himself. He is a romantic and a visionary. Leo is very idealistic and when confronted with the harshness and pettiness of the real world, can be very disillusioned. And as a fixed signed, he has difficulty accepting change.

Leo tends to be ego-centered, feeling that the world revolves around it. It may bolster its self-esteem by ingratiating itself to others.

Unfortunately, it may be willing to do anything to earn others approval. Others may use Leo's need for approval to easily coerce it.

It fears being unloved, mediocre, unappreciated and unnoticed. It can also be very shy and introverted. Leo needs to learn balance, realism and earthly wisdom; it needs to develop a sense of humor, flexibility and faith in itself.

Leo is the sign, which deals with self-confidence. It has a need for self-expression, admiration, and personal integrity. One of its main issues is learning about relationships. It has a tendency to be overly pre-occupied with itself. This can lead to egotism and arrogance. It wants to be something of real significance, to be an energy source. It is very self-expressive and needs to be accepted as such by others. It can be very dependent because of its need for approval and acknowledgment.

In conclusion, Leo is the sign, which deals with self-confidence. It has a need for self-expression, admiration, and personal integrity. One of its main issues is to learn about relationships. It has a tendency to be overly preoccupied with itself. This can lead to egotism and arrogance. It wants to be something of real significance, to be an energy source. It can be very dependent because of its need for approval and acknowledgment.

Key Words for Leo

Actor, admiration, ambitious, arrogant, autocratic, benevolent, blunt, boastful, broad-minded, candid, courageous, creative, cunning, deter-mine, devout, dignified, dignity, dominate, dramatic, expansive, extrovert, forceful, generous, glamorous, grace, grand, gullible, happy, haughty, humane, idealistic, impetuous, independent, industrious, jealous, lazy, leadership, loyal, lust for power, magnanimous, magnetic, nasty, organiz-ing, outspoken, over indulgent, overbearing, passion for luxury, persistent, philosophical, positions of command, positive, pride, prone to flattery, recognition, religious, resolute, self-assured, self-centered, self-confidence, sexual lust, showman, sincere, snobbish, splendor, spontaneous, strong will, suspicious, uncomplicated, warm-hearted.

Key Concepts for Leo

Leo represents the true search for our inner spiritual core. This sign is the major means of manifesting in material form, our inner creative urge. The goal of Leo is to help us develop confidence in ourselves through creative expressions. Leo supposed self-centeredness is really a drive towards self-recognition, not ego recognition but that, which is derived from our spiritual Source.

Besides discovery our creativity, this sign helps us to understand our life's plan or unique purpose. Leo has a strong desire to develop power, authority and of course, it's creative abilities.

Leo needs to learn to respect the needs of the larger society and the importance of one to one relationships. Leo tends to be ego-centered: it may feel that the world revolves around it. Leo needs to learn balance, realism and earthly wisdom; it needs to develop a sense of humor, flexibility and faith in itself.

Virgo is an earth and mutable sign. Its chief faculty of learning is through the senses. It is symbolized by a virgin women and is ruled by the planet Mercury.

Virgo helps us to integrate the psychological, emotional and mental components of our nature within us and in turn with our surroundings. The goal is to create a whole and complete individual through uniting both the conscious and unconscious parts of the psyche with a true and inner ordering or synthesis of our rampant desires and feelings.

This process of synthesis is as follows: first there is an inner ordering or balancing of the conscious with unconscious psyche, and in turn with mental, and psychological components; then a further synthesis of the above with physiological variables and finally an integration of a complete individual into society. This process represents the transmutation and evolution beyond just our singular identity. This allows us to experience our place in the greater scheme of things.

This process helps us to create for ourselves, a set of guidelines, rules and procedures to live by and integrate ourselves with our environment. This development of a complete individual is fostered through self-analysis, self-criticism and self-examination. Through the above, we awaken to the physical laws of nature. Through self-analysis and observation, we are able to comprehend the underlying, inherent order in the universe and within us. We are able to experience the systemic order in back of the seemingly random array of sensory impressions and stimuli. Further, we are able to synthesis this information, extracting its most usable parts.

Virgo helps us to discover the inner workings of nature and the inherent order, which exists behind what appears to be a chaotic existence. And, most important, Virgo allows us to feel that we are a part of the complex workings of the universe. Virgo is the symbol of the virgin, but not in the sexual sense.

> *"Virgo represents: the completed individual, not as Leo standing along and glorying in self, but rather confronting both the physical and social universes as an obstacle to which one must adapt, a framework through which one can learn to be effective, and a reality that must be served. It approaches the social universe in the same way."* [29]

It represents our struggle to create a whole and complete person, an individual, who is able to trust the inherent order and balance in nature

---

29: Hand, Pg. 222

and in themselves. We experience a connection or sense of community with others when we see the singularity and commonality between all of existence and us.

Through Virgo, we deal with the mundane tasks of the material world. We attend to the necessities of our physical body, our daily tasks and responsibilities in life. It helps us to create utilitarian artifacts to be used to enhance both societies and our own survival.

In conclusion, Virgo is able to both confront and unite the physical and social elements of the universe; it's path or journey is to come to some agreeable term with both. It approaches life as a series of obstacles to be met and adapted to. It is concerned with creating some type of framework or order of the universe, which in turn needs to be served. It needs social recognition for the work that it does. However, this may cause it to be overly careful and fearful of failure. It can be very insecure of itself and consequently needs the approval of others. This trend may cause it conform to the pressures of society and also to become a perfectionist. The sign creates and defines itself through work and duty. Its great achievement is through mastering implements of the world, creating worthy and dependable relationships. It is very critical of itself and others and tends to be overly analytical. It desires success and to effect changes in itself and the world. There is also a tendency to focus on details at the expense of having a grand overview and understanding of the big picture.

Key Words for Virgo

Analysis, analytical, anxious, attention to detail, care, communicator, competent, concern for health and hygiene, concerned, conscientious, critical, detail oriented, difficult relaxing, diligent, discriminating, effective, efficient, exacting, fastidious, finicky, flexible, fussy, good organizers, handle difficult tasks, hard-working, health-conscious, helpful, honest, humility, hypercritical, hypochondriac, industrious, intelligent, menial, mentally sharp, methodical, meticulous, modest, narrow, negative, no-nonsense, orderly, organize, overly structured, particular, perfectionist, petty, practical, pragmatic, precision, productive, realistic, responsible, self-analysis, self-critical, self-depreciation, self-restraint, service, servile, shy, studious, submissive. systematic, thorough, timid, trivial, un-accepting, useful, workaholic, worry.

Key Concepts for Virgo

Virgo helps us integrate the psychological, emotional and mental components of our nature. In turn, we are able to merge into the whole of society and the environment. The process is as follows: first comes an inner ordering or harmonizing of our conscious and unconscious psychic material; we then integrate this psychic arrangement with our physical needs and drives. Lastly, we integrate ourselves as complete individuals into society and our surroundings.

We are better able to understand who we are through Virgo's qualities of self-analysis, discrimination, criticism and examination. Through our own process of integration, and our striving for independence, we awakened to the physical laws of nature. Through self-analysis and observation, Virgo affords us an ability to comprehend the underlying, inherent order in the universe and in ourselves. Virgo is the symbol of the virgin, not sexually, but as one, who is not in need of another, one who is truly independent and self-sufficient.

Libra is both Air and Cardinal; the predominant faculty is the intellect. It is symbolize by the scales of Justice and is ruled by Venus.

Libra is considered the diplomat of the zodiac. As an Air sign, its emphasis is on relating to others, in this specific situation it is entering into one on one relationships. Libra interest in others can be superficial because it is relating on the intellectual level at the expense of deeply felt emotions. Libra focuses on others ideas and concepts, possibly at the expense of its own individuality.

> *"The temper is even and equitable, and if ruffled, subsidies readily. They never bear malice; in fact, the memory is inclined to be short, and there is a readiness on all occasions to forgive and forget. They fine a disturbed or quarrelsome atmosphere hard to support, and give way or compromise rather then face prolonged discord. Hence they may seem shallow and insincere".* [30]

There is a strong aesthetic quality, an appreciation of beauty. Certain specific traits are associated with Libra: cooperation, accommodation, balance and harmony. It tries to be fair and objective in all situations. Libra's chief concern is diplomacy in all of its interactions to the point where it can be indecisive. This is because of its systemic conflict between appeasing others while still maintaining its self-integrity and identity.

A major goal of Libra is achieving excellence, order and balance through overcoming the dichotomy of a secular verses divine nature. This is primarily accomplished through combining and balancing the male and female divisions within us. The inner balancing process first starts with us and then extends to our relationships. To reiterate, inner psychic balance first needs to be accomplished. This involves recognizing and honoring the assertive Yang and receptive Yin properties within us. Through the inherent diplomat characteristics of Libra, we are able, in turn, to extend this procedure in our relationship with the environment.

30: Carter, pg. 75.

> *"It (Libra) is the sign which the individual first makes an accom-*
> *modation to another individual in a one-to-one relationship, it is*
> *also a sign of aesthetic development, with a strong love of duty and*
> *harmony...it (Libra) sees in terms of polarities, I versus you, this*
> *person versus that person, we versus they. And very often for versus*
> *one may substitute together with. The key idea is that Libra cannot*
> *conceive of self in a vacuum. Self is developed only in connection*
> *with another self".* [31]

Libra is predicated upon uniting opposites, within the psyche through balancing the male—female attributes. This begins through developing an ability to love and care for ourselves. When we develop empathy and compassion, we are better able to integrate our emotions and intellect. The next logical step is extending this process outward. As we accept all facets of who we are, we become able to forgive and except others transgressions.

Libra helps us to establish a set of values based upon our subjective judgment of what we perceive as aesthetic, pleasurable and beautiful.

In conclusion, Libra can be considered a very socially oriented sign. It desires to relate to and integrate itself into a social order beyond itself. It is very apt at accommodating to another especially in a one to one relationship. It is also the sign of aesthetic development because of its powerful love of beauty and harmony. It can take the initiative but does so in a very subtle manner. It tends to define itself in relationship to another and has a difficulty with being an individual. Libra develops only in connection with other people: it is self-understanding and self-realizing in relationship to another. As an Air sign, it to has difficulty

---

31: Hand pg. 225

with intense feelings. Its approach to relationships is more on an intellectual level.

Key Words for Libra

Accommodating, adaptable, aesthetic, affection, agreeable, aloof, appearance oriented, artistic, avoids conflict, balance, careless, charming, cheerful, civil, compliant, compromising, conciliatory, contradictory, cooperative, cultured, decorum, dependent, difficult accepting reality, diplomatic, dishonest, docile, economic, elegant, evaluating, extremist, fair, flirtatious, fluctuating, focused on equality, focus on form at expensive of content, forgiveness, generous, good taste, grace, harmonious, idealistic, illusion, impartial, impressionable, indecisive, intelligent, intimate, just, lack of emotional intimacy, likable, loves beauty, mediating, modest, objective, oscillating, passive, peacemaker, peace-loving, pedantic, persuasive, phony, pleasing, poised, pretending, reasonable, reckless, refined, relationship oriented, romantic, seeking, sees self in terms of its connection with another, socially inclined, striving for balance, superficial, susceptible, sympathy, tactful, thoughtful, uncertain, unprejudiced, vacillation, vain, warm.

Key Concepts for Libra

Certain specific attributes are associated with Libra: cooperation and accommodation to other's needs, striving for balance and harmony within ourselves and in our interactions with others. Libra's primary goal is to combine and balance the male/female dichotomy. This process starts first within us and then extends outward into our relationships. The process involves combining these two opposing factions within the individual psyche and in turn combining differing factions between the environment and us. Libra, as with all Air signs, deals with relating. In this particular sign, this takes the form of developing one on one relationships. Libra is the faculty that allows one person to relate specifically to another.

Libra cannot conceive of itself living in a vacuum. Because of this need for others, we are able to further develop and individuate. Other people reflect back to us those traits we possess: through this feedback, we are able to learn much from an outside source about our identity. We are also able to experience a sense of what it is like to be a unique individual as we interact with other separate beings.

As a major learning faculty, Libra provides the ability to establish an intellectual value system based on our subjective judgment of what we find pleasurable, attractive and beautiful.

Scorpio *is both fixed and water; it represents learning on the emotional level. It is symbolized by the Scorpion and ruled by the planet Pluto.*

Scorpio is a socially oriented sign dealing with one on one relationships. But unlike Libra, which approaches them intellectually, Scorpio is relating to another on a very intense and emotionally intimate level. This sign, in its deepest symbolic sense, represents sexual union between individuals, a symbol of death of the personal ego and a merging of two souls. We are able too surrender ourselves to another, and in this process, we create a greater and more powerful entity. In this context sex is a vehicle of complete immersion into the physical realm, which transforms and transcends us above our usual limit awareness of a singular existence.

"In Scorpio and the 8th house we seek personal transformation, to overcome our separateness and become more than ourselves; we grow through our deep encounters with others and our desire to act one with them. Here we find the powerful themes of sexuality, birth, death, loss, abandonment, emotional destructiveness, rebirth and regeneration" .[32]

32: Reinhart, page 145.

Scorpio has a very strong theme of relinquishing and eliminating out-worn parts of the psyche; it tears down our structural integrity. In its deepest connotation, Scorpio represents the process of death itself, that aspect of life which includes decay, destruction, cleansing and the phenomenon of change in nature. It is analogous to the concept of Freud's thanatoes, which he used to describe the death wish as he saw it. In mythology, thanatoes is the physical being that goes around collecting the souls of the dead. Scorpio is the image of the darker or more destructive side to our nature. It is our systemic urge to destroy and die. It is analogous to the archetype of the terrible mother, one who not only can nurture, but also destroy.

> *"There is an intense emotional nature. No sign has more profound and enduring feelings, for owing to the fixity of Scorpio these become set, with the result that in high types there is unwavering, devotion to principles, deep sympathy, and true understanding, while in primitives, in whom the moral standard is low or uncertain, a host of dangerous feelings may appear—bitter dislikes or hatreds, often cherished for a lifetime, extreme sensitiveness to imagine slight or injustice, resentment, suspicion, and furious anger".* [33]

Scorpio helps mankind to better understand and accept our complete nature by helping us to incorporate its destructive side. It gives us a more comprehensive view of life including its cycles of birth, death, renewal and the knowledge that we are, at least in part, finite beings.

This most powerful and penetrating energy with its love of mystery compels us to explore our emotional and psychic depths. This helps us to better understand who we are and what motivates us. The intense penetrating qualities of Scorpio allow us to go to the very heart of any

---

33 Carter, page 75.

matter that we wish. Through this process of awakening to nature cycles our personal identity and consciousness evolves.

Scorpio allows us to access our inner core, that place which is beyond the duality of life and death. In this journey, Scorpio helps us to comprehend our finiteness. It helps us to accept our inherent destructiveness and to acknowledge that our will to destroy and die is but a part of nature. We learn to experience and accept life as a series of deaths and resurrections.

Scorpio is the key to understanding the cyclical nature of life; this helps us to endure both its destructive and benign components. Through observing this process both in nature and within us, we are better able to identify ourselves as part of the process itself. This, in turn, fosters self-understanding. Hopefully, through this particular faculty of learning, we are able to perceive and emotionally accept our mortality plus any other less savory but crucial aspects to our nature.

In conclusion, Scorpio symbolizes death of the ego. It is the merging of two individuals on a very intense emotional level. The essence of this sign is transformation especially mystical. It also represents changes that happen in ordinary reality. Scorpio is the deep immersion into the physical world rather then transcendent through the denial of ordinary reality. It views life as a series of changes and is able to see the relative nature of all things. It can observe reality at a level that is beyond the duality of bad verses good. It immerses itself into the very process of birth, death and re-birth; life is lived with great intensity and dramatic flair. Scorpio seeks out intense emotional experiences and will actually initiate them if they are not forthcoming. It has a love of mystery and a desire to explore the depths of any issue. Scorpio is highly involved in sexual exploration. The orgasm can be experienced as a vehicle for merging with another: this affords both the death of the ego and ego gratification simultaneously. Intensity is necessary in all that it experiences. It is very sensitive and easily hurt but will fight back fiercely if challenged. It has a great capacity for experiencing deep emotions. However it may not easily communicate them to others. Because of this, misunderstandings can easily occur. It usually blames itself when this lack of relating takes place. At times, it may think of itself as evil. This, in turn, can lead to secrecy, self-involvement and brooding. Scorpio can be very revengeful and can harbor feelings of hurt and resentment for a lifetime.

Key Words for Scorpio

Action, ambitious, calculating, callous, caustic, dangerous, dark, deep, destructive, devoted, dogmatic, eloquent, energetic, energy, fearless, focused, intense, intuitive, investigating, jealousy, leader, manipulative, optimistic, overly-passionate, paranoid, passionate, penetrative, pleasant, positive, principled, probing, revengeful, sarcastic, secretive, schrewd, stubborn, supportive, suspicious, tenacity, thoughtful, tyrant, vengeance, violence, will create drama for its own sake, willful, devotion.

Key Concepts for Scorpio

Scorpio helps us to incorporate the darker or more destructive sides to our nature. It represents our inherent drive for destruction and death. It helps us to recognize and accept a more encompassing picture which includes the cycle of birth, death, and renewal and the knowledge that we are, at least in part, finite beings. We are helped to experience and accept life as a series of deaths and resurrection.

Scorpio is the key to understanding the cyclical nature of life; it helps us to embrace both its destructive and benign constituents.

Sagittarius is both a mutable and Fire sign. It's predominant faculty for learning is thought the intuition. It symbolized by an archer and is ruled by the planet Jupiter.

Sagittarius has four basic goals: to confront and accept limitations imposed upon mankind by the physical world including human drives and needs; to balance individual freedom with social obligations; to create a personal system of beliefs in order to learn more about life; to comprehend patterns within nature and interconnect properties of seemingly diverse phenomenon in the environment.

Sagittarius attempts to reconcile our higher spiritual self with our mortal or human side. It helps us to balance our ideal concept of how life should be with the reality of our own imperfections and those of the world. The goal is to accept our limitations and frailties.

The method of achieving this is by developing compassion for others and ourselves, to learn to accept the way the world really is, warts and all and to learn to strike a balance between our ideal of how life should be and the reality of it.

This theme of reconciliation extends to our participation in society. There is a constant inner struggle to find an acceptable medium between our own personal needs verses our obligations to society.

Sagittarius gives us an ability to comprehend patterns and underlying systems of order behind the seemingly chaotic array of varying external stimuli. We are able to comprehend on an intuitive level the interconnection underlying the diverse experiences and events we encounter. This ability to form patterns helps us to develop greater wisdom and understanding; it affords us a deeper form of learning then if it were merely an accumulation of random and disjointed variables. We are able to formulate a personal system of beliefs or values about ourselves and our surroundings through a process of ordering our perceptions into a hierarchy of acceptable verses unacceptable factors.

As we take action in the world based upon this value and believe system, we in turn are able to change our environment; we transform and re-shape it to fit our needs. Our inherent ability to formulate belief and value systems in turn, collectively, is expressed on a social level.

Historically, this has taken the form of various systems of philosophy, law and religion.

In conclusion, its primary focus is encountering a social context and learning to understand and express itself in that setting. Sagittarius may have a difficult time balancing its own needs for freedom and self-expression versus adjusting to the restrictions of society. The solution is to be in a position in which it can express itself and be useful to society. As a fire sign, it has a difficulty in making commitments because of its need for personal freedom and self-expression. It is able to focus on the interconnections of all of existence, relating the various parts to the whole. It is very idealistic and likes to travel.

Key Words for Sagittarius

Aggressive, athletic, blunt, boisterous, brisk, buoyant, changeable, charitable, conventional, respects tradition, defiant, dependable, desire for personal liberty, desire freedom of expressing thoughts and ideas, difficult with relationships, enjoys the outdoors, exploring, extravagant, focus on abstract principles, able to detect general patterns on random stimuli, farsightedness, frankness, freedom-loving, generosity, genteel, honesty, hope, idealistic, interested in social reform, jovial, justice, kind, lawful, logical, orderly, over-confident, overly independent, perseverance, philosophical, prophecy, rash, religious, restless, sincerity, speculative, superficial, traveling, trendy, uncompromising, wandering, wise.

Key Concepts for Sagittarius:

Through Sagittarius, we are able to understand the interconnection between different experiences and events. This ability to observe patterns in nature helps us to develop greater wisdom; it provides us with a deeper form of learning then merely accumulating random and disjointed variables. Through a process of ordering our perceptions into a hierarchy of acceptable verses unacceptable factors, we are able to formulate based upon our subjective observations, a personal system of beliefs about who are and what the world is.

On a social level, our ability to create codes of conduct and belief systems is asseverated collectively through civil and religious laws.

Capricorn is both *Cardinal and earth. Its predominant faculty of learning is through the senses. This sign is symbolized by a mountain goat and is ruled by the planet Saturn.*

Capricorn interacts with the world through the senses with the specific goal of mastery the physical world. Duty and acceptance of responsibility is stressed and is played out in the arena of work. Competition, acceptance, and fulfilling one's duty are further characteristics of this sign. It helps us to focus our energy in order to fashion physical matter into concrete and utilitarian forms. Learning about material existence helps us to enhance our sense of security and safety. We become a master of some particular skill in our occupation or career. Mastery, in this connotation, denotes expertise in one's profession as oppose to using power in an authoritarian, oppressive and dictatorial fashion. In turn, we become mentors or teachers to others by sharing our knowledge.

> *"The sign of Initiation, of Cosmic Order and Justice, wherein the Individuality is developed, and humanity fulfills its obligation to others".* [34]

Capricorn represents the father principle; the embodiment of various traits that we need in order to survive: it is also the person who acted out this role in our early life. In mundane terms, this usually means resolving issues around our own biological or surrogate father.

34: Devore, pg. 372

In the deepest sense, it represents the process of developing the father principle within, a desire to learn about and model ourselves after the Father. In other words, Capricorn represents the development of our inner father, accepting our true and ultimate Source from which we originated and for whom we are vehicles of service. Developing this part of our character helps us to further define who we are. As we master the skills necessary to survive and flourish on the material plane we symbolically develop qualities associated with the father principle.

Capricorn is very ambitious and goal oriented: it focuses on structure and duty in life. It has a great respect for the material world; a strong ability to take initiative and tremendous power and ability to build and to create needed changes.

Capricorn helps us to better define and know ourselves through our relationship with the world. It helps us to learn about our identity through experiencing the limitations and practicalities of this plane.

> *"Self-preservation aggressively carried into ambition and aspiration is the key to Capricorn activity. Not content with keeping body and soul together, Capricorn must amount to something, must have some accomplishment to point to, some property to take care, of some obligation to fulfill".* [35]

It is through our experiences of limitation, frustration, difficulty, trials and tribulations that we learn to accept the inherent boundaries and parameters of this world. Through developing these specific paternal qualities within us, we are able too not only insure our survival, but also to better understand our connection with the original Source. Through this, once again we discover on the deepest of levels, our true and ultimate identity.

35: Lewi, Pg. 86

In conclusion, Capricorn is a very socially oriented sign; it tends to conform to society's pressure and criteria. It tends to define itself by community standards yet it needs to have freedom of choice and movement within those socially accepted parameters. Society rules rather than its own subjective mindset can influence it more. However, once again, the rules must be effective in practical and beneficial terms for Capricorn to follow. Although very socially concerned, it is not dependent. It needs to be in control of itself but within the acceptable parameters of social norms. It may follow society's rules and edicts but only insofar, as it is profitable to itself. It is very influenced by authority figures and is the representation of the father archetype in the world. This sign brings people out into the world and allows them to be an intricate part of society. It tends to the a bit stuffy and overly serious: it has a very difficult time to play or relax.

Key Words for Capricorn

Ability to concentrate, acceptable, accepting, achieving, ambitious, authoritarian, brooding, bureaucracy, calculating, cautious, cold, committed, conformist, conscious, conservative, controlling, cruel, crystallized, cynical, despondent, detailed, difficult to relax, diligent, domineering, driven, duty, earnest, effective, exploiting, fatal, fearful, focus on practical reality, hard-working, high-reaching, hungry for power, important, inaccessible, inhibiting, insensitive, loyal, managerial, miserly, narrow, natural, negative, obsessed with formality, overly serious, paternal, patient, persistent, pessimistic, powerful, practical, prudent, realistic, reliable, remote, repressed, reserved, resigned, responsible, rigid, rule oriented, scrupulous, security, self-containing, self-depreciation humor, self-reliance, self-sufficient, self-will, serious, severe, slow, social orientation, status-seeking, steadfast, stingy, stoic, structure, successful, suspicious, tedious, thrifty, wry.

Key Concepts for Capricorn

Capricorn interacts directly with the world through the physical senses with the specific goal of mastering the environment. It represents structure and limitations. It also deals with resolving issues situated around our own biological or surrogate father.

In a deeper sense, Capricorn represents the process of discovering the father principle within us. Through learning to master and create on the material plane, we develop qualities associated with the father. This in turn helps us to survive and flourish. Through mastering practical skills, we become more competent. Capricorn also helps us learn humility through experiencing the limitations and practicalities of the physical world.

Aquarius is both Air and a fixed energy. Its main faculty of leaning is the intellect. It is symbolized by the Water Bearer and is ruled by the planet Uranus.

Aquarius helps us to develop a social conscience. It is the rational and intellectual awareness of the interconnection of all of life and that each of us is an intricate part of it. This sign provides a holistic and global portrait of life from a detachment and intellectual perspective. Aquarius as an Air sign, is involved with relationships. However in this situation, they are on a grand social scale. We are able to develop as human beings and members of a larger aggregate. Aquarius instills us a desire to improve the future, especially through establishing ideal or utopian societies.

Aquarius has an inherent dual nature; it is both conventional and revolutionary. One facet wants order and is reactionary while the other, desires anarchy. However, both of these are equally important: one allows for society to stabilize, while the other provides change and prevents stagnation.

Another difficulty for Aquarius to resolve is balancing its need to be part of the group while simultaneously maintaining its own sense of individuality. The solution is to learn to manage this conflict in individual relationships. In this generic setting we can learn to allow our identity to remain in tack while serving the needs of another. This preparation phase can then be extrapolated to larger social situations.

Even though theoretically, Aquarius is concerned with social equality and fairness, there is a very strong egocentric component to its nature. An individual may want to make changes in society however these changes are usually predicated on ones own set of rules and ideals of how a utopian society should be. Through such characteristics as co-operation, humanitarianism, detached and fair mindedness, Aquarius continually moves forward in its quest for transformation.

Through Aquarius, we once again add to our understanding of who we are; this time, it is through group participation and the experience of being an intrinsic part of a larger order. We discover that we are social creatures, which broadens our self-definition.

This stage in our development represents the completion and dissolution of material form for all the dimensions of existence. All this is in preparation for the re-absorption of each and every entity into the original Oneness.

In conclusion, Aquarius strives to be a cooperative unit of the group: the ego and its needs are subordinate to the larger social order, at least theoretically. It can be very gregarious and enjoys social interaction. Its focus is on the social dimensions of life. As with Libra, who defines itself in contrast to another, Aquarius defines itself through social interactions. It does however have a tendency to dominate the group. In the sense it has its own style of covert egotism. It is the sign of the completely socializing ego and gains its sense of identity through it. It can also be very highly individualistic, and radically different from traditional society. Even though it is the spokesman for freedom and humanitarian ideals it has a strong desire to want to model society after its own standards and morals. It has very strong social ties yet has a difficult time with individuals. It can be the great humanitarian but has a great difficulty with one to one relationships. Aquarius has a problem with acknowledging the needs and wants of individuals. It has a fair and detached view of the world and is genuinely concerned with the good of all.

Key Words for Aquarius

Abstract, active, aloof, bizarre, brotherhood, cause-oriented, cold and logical, concerned, contrary, cooperative, cosmopolitan, criminal, detached, difficult with subjective issues, distant, earnest, eccentric, erratic, extreme, fanatic, fixed ideals, freedom loving, friendly, gregarious, gullible, humane, humanitarian, idealistic, impersonal, impractical, inflexible, intellectual, intuitive, inventive, kind, lawless, leader, mentally active, open-mind, overly analytical at expense of feelings, overly radical, patient, people-oriented, philosophical, pleasant, political, progressive, radical, rebellious, reforms, remote, revolutionary, scientific, self-willed, service oriented, sincere, socially involved. steady, stubborn, tolerant, truthful, truth seeking, unbiased, uncommitted, uninvolved, unpredictable, unprejudiced, utopian,

Key Concepts for Aquarius

Aquarius provides us with a holistic and global picture of life from a detached and intellectual perspective. As with all Air signs, Aquarius too is involved with relationships. However, in this situation, the relationships are on a grand, social scale. It is the way we develop social consciousness and an awareness of ourselves as social beings and members of a larger aggregate. Aquarius installs in us a desire to establish an ideal or utopian society. This helps all of us to move in a forward direction.

There is an inherent dual nature to this sign: it can be both conservative and rebellious. Even though theoretically, Aquarius is concerned with social equality and fairness, there is a very strong egocentric component to its nature.

Pisces is both water and mutable: the primary mode of learning is on the emotional level. It is ruled by Neptune, and is symbolized by a fish.

Pisces dissolves material form. But it also represents the beginning of a new cycle. It is symbolized by two fish arranged parallel to one another but facing in difference directions. The left side of a glyth is directed towards the beginning of a new cycle in the world of physical manifestation. The right side is directed towards evolution and the way out of the cycle of physical life. This energy as with all signs, can be expressed in various ways along a continuum: evolution through spiritual awakening, mysticism and transcendent above ego and passion all the way to defeat and failure.

Pisces is the major faculty or ability by which we can perceive our spiritual nature. It represents a direct and deep emotional experience with the Divine. This is different from an intellectual or cognitive construct of God and the spiritual realm popularized by many traditional religions. Pisces allows us to completely surrender ourselves in order to unite with our spiritual nature and the collective emotional unconscious. It represents altered states of consciousness, reality and various dimensions and possible relates to extra, sensory perception. However, Pisces can also manifest as insanity, drug addiction and lack of purposeful direction in life. It is the process of surrendering our personal will in order to re-unite with our Source of imagination and inspiration. It is our muse, our creative urge emerging from the personal and collective unconscious.

In conclusion, this water signs signals the final stage of evolution and the most difficult one because it calls for the transcendent and subordination of the self to the universe. In this process, the ego is surrendered to something higher. Its personal system of reality, morals and ethics are relinquished. This stage represents the one prior to the birth of a new self. It has a strong desire to know the ultimate truth on the spiritual level and is willing to sacrifice itself to this truth. It is very receptive and can actually take on or absorb its surroundings. It may have psychic abilities and is sensitive and receptive to those in its environment. It is capable of great compassion and empathy and is drawn to social work.

Key Words for Pisces

Apologetic, artistic, careless, compassion, concentration, creative, deceit, delicate, difficult to assert, dreamy, emotional, empathy, evasive, fantasy, good listeners, hospitality, idealistic, impressionable, indecisive, indolence, inferior complex, inspiration, lethargic, maneuvering, meditation, method, mystical, negative, order, overly receptive, overly sensitive, peace, perception, psychic, purity, refinement, religious, self-deprivation, self-pity, sensitive, service, solitude, spiritual, submissive, sunny, sympathetic, timid, vulnerable, withdrawn.

Key Concepts for Pisces

This sign's energy can be expressed in varying degrees along a continuum. It can represent evolution, spiritual awakening, mysticism and transcendence above the ego or regression, defeat and failure. Pisces can mean bless and creative inspiration but it can also manifest as insanity, addiction, and a lack of purposeful direction in life. Pisces chief function is to dissolve all material form. We are able to see beyond the illusion of Maya or form and glimpse at our true spiritual origins. It affords us the complete surrender of our personal or ego sense of self and the ability to unify with our spiritual nature and the collective emotional unconscious.

Chapter Six

Planets

On their most fundamental level, PLANETS represent various urges or dimensions of the human experience. For example, the planet Mercury symbolizes the way we become conscious or aware of the environment as well as others and ourselves. In turn Mercury orders these perceptions so they may be understood and communicated. They also represent abilities, those attributes that allow us to take action needed in this world. Again, using Mercury as an example, it is the tool or ability, which allow us to communicate and think.

Sun

"(The Sun) Reflects the individuals urge to become himself...the dot at the center (Sun glyph) suggests, that spirit, or life, or the Self, manifests itself, as an individual ego which possesses, as one of its attributes, the impulse towards Self-realization...the path which the individual must follow to fulfill his basic urge for a sense of identity". [36]

36: Greene, Liz, Relating, An Astrological Guide to Living with Others on a Small Planet (York Beach, Maine: Samuel Weiser, 1978) Pg. 30

The Sun symbolizes the heroes quest, mankind's striving for self-meaning, awareness and discovery. He represents our will, purpose, vitality and the potential we have in this lifetime. He is the symbol of the ego or personal sense of "I", the process of who we are trying to become and the path that we need to follow in order to arrive. The ego is that aspect of us, which is coherent, stable and familiar, our built in navigational system for this world. It is who we are in the here and now. It has direction, but is limited; it is born and also dies.

The Sun illuminates the other planets, which in turn, become the vehicles that help us on our journey to self-discover. It is the active transpersonal or basic energy source of which all other planets are but unique reflections. It should be remembered that the Sun is not the actual source of the vital energy, but it's focusing mechanism, the lens through which this energy is expressed. The sign the Sun is in represents the manner in which its energy is expressed and the path we are to take in order to fulfill our potential in this lifetime. Each planet represents a unique frequency or pattern of energy of the Sun; they are the tools that help us on our quest for self-awareness.

The movement of the planets, which again reflects the Sun's energy, each in their own unique fashion, creates constant change. Through this continual process we are able to define and re-define ourselves through-out our lifetime. The journey of the Sun allows us to discover our meaning in life, to have an awareness of our own existence. The Sun is mankind's drive to unify all the varying dimensions of himself through transcending and overcoming nature's inherent duality. He is the path on which we search for and consequently reunited with our true Source. The ultimate goal in this process is to attain a state of Nirvana. The Sun is the vehicle which allows us to do just that.

The journey itself may be a universal human experience, but the specifics, the type of experiences we encounter along the way, are wholly personal and unique to each one of us. Through the Sun, we are constantly discovering our life's path. This is accomplished through making conscious choices, which effects us on a daily bases. He is also the source of our creative potential and personal will manifested in the form of the ego.

The Sun is the active guiding male principle, our essential or core self. He is our power source, and our very will to live. The overall goal is to develop all of our resources, which are symbolized through the specific placements of the planets in our chart. Through transcending above all personal concerns, bias and aspirations we are able to rediscover our true spiritual essence. We are able to move beyond our desires, longings and ambitions.

In conclusion, the Sun helps us to evolve into our true and ultimate self; he is the symbol of wholeness and the impulse towards self-realization. The sign that the Sun is in, is the path, which we must follow in order to achieve this goal. He helps us to cultivate our ability to express ourselves and to be come self-aware. Once again, the sign that the Sun is in represents qualities that we can potentially actualize into our conscious state. The goals, which are symbolized by this sign, become part of our aspirations in life. For example, if the Sun were placed in the sign of Leo, pride, creativity and a desire for recognition would be an important part of our makeup. We would need to cultivate a great many of those the characteristics associated with Leo in order to evolve. We are not inherently ruled by a particular sign, regardless of what the Sun sign columnist might like us to believe; instead, we need to utilize the attributes associated with a particular sign in order to grow. It involves a life long process of unfolding. The placement of our Sun in the natal chart denotes where the greatest effort in creating this very sense of personal identity takes place. For example, if the Sun were in the tenth house, career and public recognition would be a priority. The Sun is the masculine and active principle or the Yang. He also symbolizes the father. He concerns himself with individual will, consciousness and decision making abilities.

Key Words for the Sun

Ambitious, animalistic, arrogant, basic energy of being, center, life giving, centering, consciousness, constructive, core, creative, democratic, despotic, dignified, father principal, fountainhead of all life, independent, individualization, integration, integrity, lacking ambition, lazy, leadership and authority, life force, life-giving energy, life's potential, loving pride, males in one's life, masculine, ostentatious, over emphasis on form at expense of quality, personal power, personality or ego, physical energy, pompous, principal of self-actualization, purpose, radiant, self-actualization, strives for education, the Hero, versatile, vitality, will power, will, Yang.

Key Concepts for the Sun

The Sun symbolizes the Heroes Quest, the striving towards self-meaning, awareness, and discovery. He is the basic energy source of which all other planets are but unique reflections. Each planet represents a unique frequency or pattern of energy of the Sun: they are the tools that help us on our venture.

It is the constant movement of the planets that keeps life flexible and in a constant state of change. Because of this, we are able to learn, through the various experiences we encounter, who we are, our true identity as represented through the sign the Sun is in. On a personal level, he is also the source of our primal creative potential and will.

Moon

> "*The Sun reflects the urge within every human being to express himself, and grow into what he potentially is. The Moon, in contrast, symbolizes the urge towards unconsciousness, toward the past, and towards immersion in the flow of feelings which allows the*

individual to be part of the mass current without undertaking the requirement for self-consciousness". [37]

The Sun is the source of our spiritual nature while the Moon represents our physical existence. She is the stage where upon the dance in the dream of material existence plays out. It is where we act out the rediscovery of who we are, our own personal passion play, if you will. This drama of sleep represents a retreat back to the primal unity.

The Moon is our experience of union on a conscious level with the three dimensional world of physical form. It is our experience of a sense of belonging, of feeling apart of the physical realm. She is our maternal lineage, the influence of the one who played the mother role in our early life. As the foundation of our physical being, the Moon is our ability to feel comfortable within our own skin. She represents our automatic reaction patterns and adjustment to physical stimuli. She is the unconscious conditioned emotional behavior learned in early childhood. The Moon is the source of our emotions, including moods and habits on the most primal levels that allows us to adapt to our environment. Our emotional faculties help us to feel that we are a part of the biological order and to connect to others and the environment.

The Moon represents our material body, the vessel or container (um vase) through which we experience boundaries and limitations. She helps us accept our inclusive physical needs, wants, desires and appetites.

Because we experience fluctuations in our emotions, we are able to relate to the cycles of change in material existence; further we are able to sense that we too are a part of the cyclical nature of life. The moon is responsible for the development of habits, which are the ordering, and repetition of behavioral patterns either consciously or unconsciously.

37: Ibid. Pg. 33

They are formed out of the basic need for security. On the most primal level, it is our response to other people and the environment in general.

The Moon is the symbol of nourishment; the substance from this physical realm needed to sustain physical life. She is the mother figure or Magna Madre (Great Mother) who nurtures and gives birth. She also provides the womb or structure from where this birth takes place. She is the symbol of the breast but can be both nurturing and volatile, beneficial and ambivalent, enveloping, dangerous and multiplicitous. In her capacity as prime mother, she can also be experienced as a destroyer, the terrible mother: she is one who can both nurture and but also destroy. It is from our earliest experiences with this maternal figure, that we develop either a trust or mistrust in life and the ability or inability to provide for ourselves in this world. She is actively involved in reproduction and is the symbol of conception specific to fertilization. Because she represents the world of appearances and imagination, we may experience errors in understanding and comprehending at times.

She is the seat of our natural instincts, the principle that allows us to care for our body through the ability to satisfy our appetites and manage our survival needs. She is the source of emotional guidance and represents our desire to be nurtured and nurture in return.

The Moon deals with our ability to emotionally relate to other people. This provides us both security and assures our survival and that of societies. In essence, she is responsible for both social cohesiveness and personal survival. The Moon is responsible for feelings of inner contentment, safety and security through assisting us in satiating our appetites and desires. Through her, it is possible for us to feel we are at home, being taken care of, understood and belong.

In conclusion, while the Sun represents the male or active principal in life, the Moon is feminine and receptive. She is our drive towards the unconscious, the past, and immersion into the flow of feelings. She is the mother principle, the womb or retreat and our desire to seek security and safety. Her locality in our natal chart, is where we surrender into the practice of living without having to necessarily understand what we are experiencing. Here is where we seek safety, refuge and escape. The Moon is the desire for comfort and satisfaction of our emotional needs. She wants to take us back to our instinctual and non-rational nature. It is where we are most dominated by our instinctual needs rather than relying on our own will and decision making capacity. The sign the Moon is in represents these instinctual needs. They need to be acknowledged for our emotional well being. For example, if the Moon were in the sign of Cancer, to nurture and be nurtured that is some type of mothering role and emotional connection with others would be an instinctual part of our subconscious disposition.

Key Words for the Moon

Ability to adapt to new situations, agreeable, automatic response to stimuli, body, capricious, childhood, container, content, domestic affairs, domestic, emotional reflexes, environment, family matters, feelings, emotions, feminine, fixed patterns, flowing, frivolous, fruitful, heredity, heritage, home, homeland, inaccurate, inconsistent, indolence, inherited emotional patterns, inhibited, insecure, instincts, lazy, maternal, matrix, medium, moods, mother, motherhood, nocturnal, overly sensitive, passive, peace loving, personal past, practical affairs, principal of change, procrastinate, psychic perceptions, psychological patterns, quiet, reactions, receptive, respond, restless, serene, tender, timid, unconscious assumptions, uninterested, vulgar, weak, womb, women, Yin.

Key Concepts for the Moon

The Sun is the source of our spiritual nature while the Moon represents our physical existence. The Moon is our experience of union on a conscious level with the three dimensional world of physical form. It is the symbol of our sense of belonging and feeling a part of physical reality.

The Moon represents our material body, the vessel or container (um vase) through which we experience boundaries and limitations. She helps us except our inclusive physical needs wants, desires, and appetites.

The Moon is the symbol of nourishment; the substance from our universe needed to sustain physical life. She is the mother figure or Magna Madre (Great mother) who gives birth and nurtures all.

The Moon deals with our ability to relate emotionally to other people. She is responsible for feelings of inner contentment, safety, and security through helping us to successfully satisfying our appetites and desires.

Mercury

> "Thinking, reflecting, analyzing and exchanging ideas are processes ascribed to Mercury by traditional astrology and reason by modern psychology as an expression of an instinctive behavior pattern that, like all other archetypes factors, is present in each one of us." [38]

Mercury, in Roman mythology, is the messenger of the gods. He is also the god of purchasing and trading. He shares many of the same traits as that of the Greek god Hermes.

Mercury serves dual functions: first he assimilates information and second, communicates it. He represents the process of perceiving, recognizing and categorizing, then placing this random array of incoming stimuli into some type of meaningful pattern. This takes place in both the conscious and unconscious levels of our psyche.

38: Hamaker-Zondag, Pg. 54

Mercury helps us to perceive such characteristics in the environment as color, weight, size and form. The random information from our surroundings is taken in through all of our sensory faculties: intuition, senses, emotions and intellect. We are able to ascribe meaning to the data by creating patterns of interrelationships on a variety of conscious levels.

Hermes served as an agent who conducted the souls of the dead to the underworld. This metaphorically represents the journey that Mercury takes us on. He helps us along the voyage into the inner recesses of our sub-conscious. But unlike the one way journey of the Hermes figure, the information we gather is also transported back to the surface or level of consciousness. It is a symbolic type of resurrection. Mercury serves as a unifying agent between varying sub-strata: it is able to link our conscious, personal unconscious with the collective unconscious. It is the tool, which affords us access to information that was previously repressed.

Mercury represents communication, either in spoken or written form. This includes all types of symbols that fostered an exchange of ideas, experiences, emotions and insights. One of the major characteristics, which separates us from the animal kingdom is our ability as humans to differentiate ourselves from that which we observe. We develop our sense of singular identity through our awareness of being separate from our surroundings. It is through our relationship with the "not-I" that we experience our sense of uniqueness and develop an awareness of ourselves as an "I".

Through the actions of Mercury, we assimilate knowledge. This expands our self-awareness and our recognition of ourselves as separate beings. Through the ability to change and maintained a degree of flexibility and dexterity in our lives, we keep evolving. Mercury aids us in handling change. Because of the influx of information we are able to constantly re-evaluate our beliefs, attitudes and convictions about life and ourselves.

In conclusion, Mercury can be classified a neutral energy. It is the way we perceive and order our perceptions in such a way that we can both understand and communicate them. It is our urge to understand and integrate unconscious motives with conscious recognition. It is not merely the intellect because we can also perceive and comprehend through our feeling nature and intuition. The sign position indicates the best way in which we many learn. For example, if Mercury is situated in the sign of Cancer, we discern or take in information through the unconscious and in turn evaluate it through our feeling nature. It is the way through which we become conscious of our surroundings, as well as ourselves. It is the desire to digest experiences, to become aware of the world around us. The house position of Mercury indicates where we both learn the greatest amount and the area in life that we are most interested in.

Key Words for Mercury

Ability to adapt, alert, analytical, articulate what is the truth, brilliant, clever, clumsy, communication, conceded, connecting, co-workers, cunning, decision-making ability, detail, dexterity, diplomat, eloquent, fanciful, forgetful, formulated ideas, imaginative, impressionable, inconsistent, industrious, ingenious, inquisitorial, intellectual, literate, logic and reason, logos, mediating, mental, mind, movement, neighbors, nervous, one-sided communication, overly critical, perceiving, petty, physical dexterity, pleasing, profane, rationalizes, reasoning, restless, retention, routine travel, sensitive, short trips, shrewd, siblings, skepticism, skillful, subtle, symbol-making, the mind, thinking process, translation, transportation, tricky, understanding, verbose, versatile, witty, worrying, youthful.

Key Concepts for Mercury

Mercury, in Roman mythology, is the messenger of the gods. It assimilates and orders information into some form of comprehensive sequence and then communicates it either through speech or in written form. We input this information through all of our inherent learning faculties: intuition, senses, emotions, and intellect. This process of categorizing takes placed on both an unconscious and conscious psychic level. Mercury also helps us to distinguish color, weight, size, and form in the environment.

Venus

> *"We also have, in Venus, the entering into relationships on basis of mutual dependency, the maintenance of those and harmony in relations by mutual respect and recognition, and the already mentioned unity of opposites, by which the Venus function becomes the power source becoming expressions of love and affection".* [39]

Venus represents Eros, the life affirming principle. She affords us the opportunity to discover the power of love and union with others. She helps us to find similar qualities in what might appear at first as opposites and in turn, we discover what is valuable in each.

Venus is the ability to abandon ourselves into our desires and passions. She is a receptive force through which we are able to sort through our experiences and establish a criterion of what we find is satisfactory and pleasurable or not. As we learn what makes us happy, what we experiencing as pleasurable, we are able to create a subjective value system.

---

39 Ibid. Pg. 155

We are able to experience a spontaneous response to our passions and pleasures through abandoning ourselves to these choices. Further, as we learn to value and appreciate ourselves; we, in turn, feel worthier of success and of acquiring the necessary material support we need in this world. We learn to appreciate our own power of attraction. We become aware of what we want and through this process come to understand what we truly value.

In the process of giving ourselves to another, we discover. our inherent worth. We are able to choose a partner based on characteristics that we find valuable in another. Although our attempts to choose the appropriate partner are disappointing at times, we are exercising our own free will. Choosing a partner or anything that we consider of great value is an inherent act of self-identity because we are making unique choices that reflect our personal values. In turn, through this process, we enhance our knowledge and self-awareness. We build a more enlightened definition of who we are. Further, as two complete individuals merge, there union creates a more inclusive and expanded entity. This singleton is inherently greater than just the sum of its parts.

Venus helps us to develop balance within our relationships: we are able to have respect and gain recognition for others and ourselves as unique beings. The other person is a source of reflective energy, mirroring back to us our essential characteristics.

Further, through our union with another, we are able to experience and respect the great power inherent in love. We become more inclusive individuals because we exercise our ability to choose.

Through our awareness of erotic and sexual feelings and our capacity for pleasure, we are able to create a personal value system. This process separates us from the bonds of our childhood and parents. Erotic feelings denote our arrival into adulthood. Through maintaining our body as a source of pleasure, beauty and satisfaction, we are better able to accept ourselves. In turn, we concede that we are worthy of enjoyment and fulfillment.

In conclusion, Venus gives us permission to enjoy pleasure. She is our desire to relate, harmonize and adjust to personal relationships. She represents values, personal taste, and qualities sought in our ideal partner. She wishes to be desired and experience the type of recognition that comes from having a special partner. She is our image of what is loved and considered beneficial; Venus is our disposition towards love, relationships and social intercourse. She is the energy used to seek out others with similar tastes and interests. Through her we discover the similarities or common ground which exists among people. She represents the give and take, live and let live axiom in nature. Venus is the symbol of the lover; she represents womanhood. For both sexes, she symbolizes how we give and receive love and affection.

Key Words for Venus

Affection, amiable, loving, artistic, attraction, beautiful, benign, cheerful, clean, close relationships. compassionate, courteous, delicate, elegant, independent, erotic, feminine, flirtatious, frivolous, gentle, graceful, indolence, indulgent, kind, lazy, lenient, loving, luxurious, modest, nourishing, peaceful, pleasing, poetic, refined, regal, rejoicing, sensual, social, sympathetic, tame, tender, warm, yielding, greed, emotionally demanding, generous, giving, harmony, bonding, attraction, marriage, partnership, romantic attractions, luxury, valuable, personal possessions, attractions, refinement, vanity, retention, ostentatious, indulgent, Yin.

Key Concepts for Venus

Venus exemplifies our ability to abandon or merge ourselves into our desires and passions. She helps us to learn what makes us happy and to discover what experiences give us pleasure. Because of this knowledge we are able to create an esoteric value system based on what we like or dislike. For example, choosing a partner or anything that we consider of great worth is an inherent act of self-identity because we are making unique decisions that reflect our personal values. We become more inclusive individuals, when we use our free will to make choices in our lives.

Mars

> "*Mars represents your methods, your techniques, your approach, towards a goal systematically...Mars also shows how one expresses desires and how one asserts oneself, especially by its sign position. Not just passionate desires either, but how in general you express what you want. Mars is about trying to get your desires fulfilled too; again it's your method of going after something*". [40]

Mars is the archetype principle representing aggression and passion, including sexual. He helps us to maintain our sense of uniqueness especially when we are in social situations. As a remnant of our more primitive nature, he is one of our main survival mechanisms. When we are in a situation that poses danger, the fight or flight principle is activated; we either choose to take a stand and fight or leave the situation as quickly as possible.

Mars helps us to stand up for ourselves, to be our own advocate. He helps us to define who we are based on what we want in life. Further, we are able to develop a sense of identity through acquiring new skills and learning to rely on our own initiative. We become aware of our own autonomy. We are capable of thinking and acting independently. Mars is the mechanism by which we separate from the universe at large and define ourselves as individuals. He represents our ability for self-reliance,

40: Sasportus, Page 111.

independence, and self-determination and to achieve our goals. He helps us to cultivate freedom in all parts of our lives.

Venus represents integration while Mars is the principal that represents segregation or separation of reality into various divergent components. Mars emphasizes the inherent differences rather than similarities in life. He furnishes us with energy to initiate action in the world; he represents kinetic movement, which allows for agility and locomotor activity.

Mars is raw sexual impulse, the sex drive and possibly the very act of sexual union itself. He does not however include the experience of the orgasm. In general, there is a very strong theme of insemination and proliferation, not only on the biological level but also symbolically, by helping us to define ourselves as unique beings. He represents the process of self-creation on a continual basis.

In conclusion, this planet is the counterpoint to Venus. He is the drive towards conquest, segregation and separation. He represents the manner in which we assert and go about fulfilling our needs in life. We are able to experience ourselves as different and unique from others whenever we assert our needs and wishes. He is the way we go after what we want in life, the manner in which we strive to get our desires met including sexual.

Key Words for Mars

Abusive, accident, action, adventurous, aggressive, anger, antithesis, antagonists, boastful, bold, brave, business ambition, caustic, combative, courage, criminal, daring, defiance, desire, destructive, direct, disruptive, energetic, enterprising, exciting, expert, fever, fiery, fight or flight reaction, forcefully, furious, gallant, high-spirited, hostile, energetic, impulsive, infantile, initiation, initiative, invincible, irritation, kinetic, loud, magnanimous, masculine, military, motion, muscular, obscene, obstinate, oppressive, passionate, physical energy, physical exertion, quarrelsome, quick, reckless, resourceful, rough, segregation, self-center, sensual, separation, sexual, survival, temper, turbulent, use of force or threat, vigor, violent, willful, will-power, Yang.

Key Concepts for Mars

Mars is the universal principle representing aggression and passion, including sexual. He helps us to maintain our sense of uniqueness especially when we are in a social setting. Mars also symbolizes the flight or fight principal. Venus is the energy that represents integration, while Mars stands for segregation or separation of reality into divergent segments. He emphasizes the inherent differences rather than similarities in life. Mars is raw sexual impulse, the sex drive and possibly the very act of sexual union itself.

Jupiter

> "In this way Jupiter is truly a god of the gateway, for he forms a link between conscious and unconscious through the creation and intuitive understanding of symbols. As we have seen, symbols are the primordial language of life; and Jupiter symbolizes the function which both creates them within men and intuits their meaning". [41]

Jupiter personifies success, achievement, luck, expansion, ingesting, and integration. He represents any process that tends to increase or extend. We expand our psyche, increase our range of motion by venturing out into the world and incorporating into us as much of it as possi-

---

41: Greene, Liz, Relating, An Astrological Guide to Living with Others on a Small Planet (York Beach, Maine: Samuel Weiser, 1978) Pg. 41

ble. He is growth, both psychologically and physical. Through him we learn to master and attune ourselves with the external world.

He helps us to overcome challenges. Jupiter in conjunction with the Moon supports us in our quest for emotional well being and instills in us such characteristics as nobility, justice, generosity, and piety.

Through him, we grow and improve: he is the principal of expansion, the urge to develop faith, trust and confidence in the world and in ourselves. We develop a sense of openness to life and learn to trust that the universe will care for us.

As the ruler of Sagittarius, Jupiter is related to the principle of integration. He helps us to orchestrate incoming data by converting the information into meaningful symbols, which makes the information meaningful to us.

As we can see, one of Jupiter's main functions is to provide mankind with the ability and desire to form symbols. In this way we not only can communicate with one another, but between the various levels of consciousness within our psyche. We expand our consciousness and in turn feel that we are truly a part of creation. We are capable of overcoming our sense of alienation and separation. We realize that everything has its place in the scheme of life. Through Jupiter, we come to understand that we too are part of that scheme, a part of something that is greater than just who we are as individuals. We are able to gain a broader perspective on life and view it on a grander scale. Because of this sense of unity, we, in turn, are driven to seek and understand the deeper meanings of life. As the knowledge we acquire is integrated, we develop the capacity to form conscious judgments about our existence. On a collective social level, this process of ingestion and integrating information expresses itself through a variety of philosophical and religious social constructs.

Through our capacity for self-dignity, open mindedness, broadened vision, improved ability to make judgments and common sense, we are able to be of greater service both to society and to ourselves.

In conclusion, Jupiter is how we seek to grow, mature and flourish. He is our ability to comprehend patterns or symbols in nature. These symbols tell us that there is some type of intrinsic order or meaning to the universe. The sign and house that Jupiter is in suggests the route through which we can experience this sense of unity. He is also our ability to create symbols. He is involved in our dream world. He is the link between our conscious and unconscious psyche through the symbols presented to us while we sleep. We derive our intuitive understanding of archetypes and patterns through him.

Key Words for Jupiter

Abundant, adventurous, affluent, arrogant, auspices, autonomy, benevolent, benific, broad overview, careless, charitable, compensation, conceded, correct, creation of a larger frame of reference, cultural awareness, digestion, dissipated, enthusiasm, excessive, exorbitant, expansive, exploration, extravagant, faith, fanatical, gluttonous, good luck, growth, guru, higher education, honest, honorable, hospitable, humorous, illicit, immense, increase, indulgent, ingesting, integration, irresolute, irresponsible, jovial, judicious, just, lavish, lazy, learning, long journeys, long range plans, noble, openness to grace, opportunity, optimism, over confidence, over-promises, patient, peaceful, philanthropic, philosophical, preservation, procrastinate, prosperity, rational, reckless, religious, respectful, scattered energy, self-indulgent, self-sustaining, success, sympathetic, tactful, trust in higher power, truthful, valuable, wise.

Key Concepts for Jupiter

Jupiter personifies success, achievement, luck, expansion, gestation, and integration. In conjunction with the Moon, He helps us to achieved a sense of emotional well being and installs in us a variety of such positive attributes as nobility, justice, generosity, and piety to name but a few. He is the principal of expansion, the urge to develop faith, trust and confidence in the world and in ourselves. Through him, we cultivate openness to life and learn to trust that the universe can sustain and support us. Jupiter assists us in overcoming our inherent feelings of alienation and separation.

He represents our drive for information and our ability to add to and build upon the knowledge we already possess. Through this process, we develop the capacity to make conscious judgments about life.

Saturn

> *"Saturn symbolizes the collective social aspects of life. He is responsible for making rules, setting limits and providing the foundation upon which social and material reality is built".*

Saturn represents form, structure and social stability through laws and cultural traditions. He is the collective will of the people specifically expressed in a social context. Saturn represents our limitations and boundaries in this world of form. He is responsible for three-dimensional reality. He provides structure to what would otherwise be complete chaos.

We experience negative consequences if we do not recognize and respect our limitations or play, as it were, within acceptable parameters. This is the true meaning of the term law: all action has it consequences. Reality is basically recognizing limitations; choosing some parts while excluding others. He helps us to learn discipline and responsibility for our personal actions. Saturn is the symbol of the father, the one who makes rules for our own safety. Through hard work and vigilance, we learn what we need to function and be productive in this world. He is the principle of self-preservation, personal integrity and structure.

Saturn provides us with a moral center or compass, an internal socializing mechanism, which helps us to learn what is socially acceptable or not.

He is associated with the shadow or so-called unacceptable parts of us that we tend to fear. However if we block the expression of these traits, we may later experience them in the form of guilt and shame. Through our conscious ego, we are able to recognize the consequences of our actions. We make future decisions and act responsibly based on what we have learned.

Although painful at times, Saturn points out our imperfections and areas of greatest vulnerability. Through the experience of pain, limitation and discipline we are better able to mature and develop greater awareness and accept all facets of our character. Our energy is blocked or restricted in the house of our natal chart where Saturn resides. This house represents the area of our greatest weakness and lack of confidence: it is our Achilles heal. It is also where we may try too hard to succeed. We tend to regard it as overly important. Through self-analysis and eventual acceptance of our frailties, we become more integrated, whole and complete. He represents ambition and tenacity; Saturn urges us onward towards our goals; we are able to become wiser, more realistic and have a clearer picture of life through learning from our mistakes. Part of the process of defining who we are is based on learning from hard knocks, experiencing guilt, grief, inadequacy, delay and disappointment. Sometimes, through what may seem harsh, we learn to better ourselves.

Through Saturn lessons, we are able to move beyond any overly intense self-involvement. Through his influence, we are able to create a more realistic and enduring self-identity based not on self-delusion or ego-inflation but on practical accomplishments and through witnessing the immediate results of our actions. We build up confidence through observing the fruits of our labor, the direct results of our actions. Saturn represents the method by which we establish and preserve ourselves through sustained effort: he represents our urge to defend our psychological, emotional and physical integrity. By learning to rely upon our own resources and using time more productively, we become more self-sufficient and reliant.

Saturn lessons can be compared to those of Pluto (see Pluto section). He deals with painful yet necessary experiences and like Pluto, Saturn is allied with the darker sides of humanity. However, while Pluto represents raw power, destruction, and decay, Saturn deals with the actual limitations we experience in life, the boundaries we all come up against.

Key Words for Saturn

Accurate, ambitious, authority, avarice, barrier, boss, cold, concrete, confined, conservative, contraction, control, conventional, creation of form, cultural traditions, defensive, definition, delay, diligent, directed effort, discipline, fatalist, frustration, hard worker, harsh, holds in, inadequate, inflexible, integrity. intense, introspective, isolation, law, limitations, limits, loyalty, one's internal father, order, patient, perseverance, pessimistic, proficient, prudent, realistic, regulation, reserved, responsibility, restrain, restrictions, rigid, self-conscious, self-control, self-denial, self-discipline, self-preservation, sense of duty, sense of justice, serious, shape, skeptical, sober, social consequences, social structure, solid, sorrow, structure, sublimating, suspicious, sustained, tack, teacher, tenacity, thrift, tradition, urge for security.

Key Concepts for Saturn

Saturn symbolizes the collective social aspects of life. Our experience of reality, which he represents, is based on our attention to certain elements in the environment while excluding others.

As our super-ego, he helps us to learn discipline and responsibility for our personal actions. We are better able to make future decisions based on what we have already learned from our past. Reality is based on a process of learning through hard knocks, experiencing guilt, grief, inadequacy, delay and disappointment.

Through Saturn's lessons, we are able to move beyond any overly intense self-involvement. He represents the method by which we establish and preserve ourselves through sustained effort: he represents our urge to defend our psychological, emotional and physical integrity or perimeters.

While Pluto represents raw power, destruction, and the process of decay, Saturn is more associated with the actual limitations we experience in life, the boundaries we all come up against.

Uranus

> "Uranus, the great Awakener, prevents stagnation: is the catalyst for change, progress and innovation".

He strikes with lightning like speed. Change is experienced in quantum leaps, sometimes erratic and unsettling. The changes may produce a mutation, radically different from the norm. Ideas may come to us as brilliant flashes of insight and awareness. They may be experienced in the form of a Gestalt, or spontaneous and complete comprehension of a situation in a new and novel manner. Uranus helps us to explore uncharted regions of the mind, to access the unconscious and collective unconscious. Suddenly hidden or suppressed material of the unconscious surfaces generating new and innovative ideas.

This process adds to our personal sense of uniqueness and provides new solutions to old problems through paradigm shifts in our thinking. We are able to scrutinize data in a detached, objective and scientific like manner.

Uranus's curiosity, experimental nature and liberal attitudes also extend into the sexual arena. It is through this energy, that society's morays, especially sexual, are constantly shifting to reflect the subconscious needs of its members. On an individual basis, a person who has a high degree of Uranus in their chart tends to have a more liberal view on this subject and may act out accordingly.

Altruistic, Uranus participates in social reform. There is a strong desire to stand out, as it were, from the crowd. He prides himself in being unique and different from conventional society's norms and social standards. Although he is the humanitarian champion of the underdog, Uranus wishes to transform society in his own image and likeness. His desire for progress is somewhat ego-center. In its most extreme manifestation, he can create a very cold, calculating, and efficient social machine void of emotion and compassion. Progress is initiated usually at the expense of individual rights and freedoms. Change can evolve into dogma of political correctness taken to the extreme. We can witness this, for example, in such modern day atrocities as: the killing fields of Cambodia; Stalin's Russian, Hitler's Nazis Germany; and to a lesser extent, the McCarthy era of the '50s in the United States.

Uranus can manifest itself as the extreme version of the male or Yang archetype, a cold and cruel figure that rules without compassion or mercy. The solution is to balance the needs of society and those of its citizens.

Uranus is a malleable energy that prevents stagnation, entropy and removes outworn attitudes and mental construct both on an individual and societal level. We are able to let go of established norms, customs and morays assuring new and continuing growth. Through him we are given the opportunity to experience ourselves as vessels of change, awareness and expanded consciousness. He is the spirit of independence, autonomy and self-reliance. He fosters an intellectual desire for freedom and independence of thought and action.

In conclusion, he represents the world of collective ideas i.e. those that we all share as a common species. He is the urge to break free of our identification with material reality and to experience the wonders of the universal mind. Uranus symbolizes change, disruption, freedom, invention, the unconventional, and liberation. He is our incentive to broaden our knowledge beyond mere concrete existence. On an intellectual level, we begin to understand how all of life fits into a pattern or scheme. This realization usually is experienced as flashes of insight. He is our desire to upgrade from our limited understanding of the world to one that is much more comprehensive.

Key Words for Uranus

Abnormal, abrupt, acute, adventurous, anarchist, fanatic, archetypes, astrology, audacious, awaken, breakthrough, calculating, change, chaotic, cold, Collective Unconscious, instant need for change and excitement, contrary, cooperative, defiant, desire to break free, detachment, developments, dictatorial, disruptive situations, disruptive, drastic, eccentric, electric, electronics, energized, illumination, enthusiasm, erratic, event, experimental, explosive, extremist, fanatical, fascist, flashes of insight, freedom, genius, groups, heroic, humanitarian, idealistic, impatient, impersonal, independent, ingenious, innovative, instability, intuitive, irresponsible, isolated, lawless, liberal, light, lightning like, liberation, magnetic, modern, new ideas, occult, organizations, original conceptions, original, peculiar, perverse, philosophical, progressive, prophetic, quaint, radical, random, rapid alteration of consciousness, rebellious, reformation, rejecting, respect for freedom, restless, reverse, revolution, sarcasm, scientific, section, self-centered, self-will, sense of freedom, spasmodic, sudden, technology, telepathic, transformation, truth, turbulent, uncentered, unconventional, underlying patterns of collective thought, unexpected, unfocused, Universal Mind, unusual events, unusual, utopian, vibrant, will, willful, wisdom.

Key Concepts for Uranus

Uranus, also known as the great Awakener, is the catalyst for change, progress, and innovation: because of this, he is the energy that prevents stagnation. His actions are sudden, unexpected, and can be drastic. The changes he produces are mutations, which are radically different from the norm. Uranus helps us to explore uncharted regions of the mind and allows us to access the personal and collective unconscious. We are able to enter the pool of conscious and unconscious mental processes and activities. His curiosity, experimental nature and liberal attitudes also extend into the sexual arena.

Uranus wants to participate in social reform. However, he fancies to create a political structure based on his image of a utopian society.

Uranus is a malleable energy, one that sanctions change in the universe. He prevents stagnation, entropy, and removes outworn attitudes and mental constructs both on an individual and societal level.

Neptune

> *"The world, is not as it is in itself but as we perceive it and react upon it, is the product of our own Maya or delusion. It can be described as our own more or less blind life-energy, producing and projecting demoniac or beneficial shapes and appearances. Thus we are the captives of our own Maya-Shakti, of the motion picture that this incessantly produces".* [42]

Neptune is responsible for producing change on the deepest of emotional levels through disintegration and separation. His energy is analogous to salt water, like a corrosive solvent, its action is slow but

---

42: Hand, Pg. 206

steady. On an inter-psychic level, he dissolves our defense mechanisms, allowing unconscious material to surface. He is the manner by which we search for our true spiritual identity. Neptune erodes our sense of personal individuality, disintegrates and separates us from our peripheral self. Neptune can be compared to the ocean that is comprised of two basic principles: ceaseless movement and formlessness, the basic dynamic forces and transitional states of universal life. The ocean symbolizes both fertility and sterility due to the destructive nature of salt water. And like the ocean with its uncharted regions, Neptune represents the uncharted dimensions of human consciousness. He represents both the illusion of and the path through the mirage of which is material existence.

Neptune denotes our desire to return to the womb, to the Source of Oneness with God: he is our desire to return to Eden, our longing to journey back home. This may be experienced as a type of systemic, existential homesickness.

Neptune blurs the line between finite and infinite, between the material and spiritual realms of existence. One might say that Neptune is the agent of our true spiritual reality. He helps us to break through the world of illusion or Maya.

Neptune is our desire for Nirvana, the experience of nothingness. It is the mystic state that is the ecstasy of self-annihilation and the absence of conflict and contrast. It is a state of consciousness beyond the illusion of duality.

Neptune is a unifying agent, who dissolves the barriers between the conscious and personal unconscious and collective unconscious. He is the principal of the mystic and represents that which is outside of time and space. We are able to access the spiritual world, which in turn enhances our sense of individuality. We are able to experience that part of us, which is able to relinquish our personal ego in the service of the collective. We are afforded compassion and a sense of unity with something greater than just who we are.

"Neptune symbolizes the truth and divinity perceived by the mystics...at the highest level, Neptune represents Nirvana, where all individuality is merged into an infinite oneness of being and consciousness...in the presents of Neptune, the illusion of the ego becomes clear". [43]

As the universal creative impulse manifested in the material world, he is the source of our artistic inspiration. He guides us to the state of perfection, to the ultimate truth, and to a direct experience with the Divine. In a sense, he represents the very depths of our subconscious, the energy that unleashes storms and passions of the soul.

As representative of the ideal nature of mankind, he carries a Trident or three-pointed spear. This weapon symbolizes the perversion of the three main drives of man: preservation becomes possession or covetousness; reproduction becomes lust and the drive for spirituality becomes vanity.

As the higher octave of Venus, his love encompasses all of humanity and creation. He is source of devotion and unconditional, universal love. He is the inherent principle of oneness of all creation. He represents freedom from the world of material form and escape from our prison of isolation.

There are inherent dangers in the quest for spiritual enlightenment. One may loss touch with material reality. For some, it can take the form of drug or alcohol abuse, loss of direction in life or even insanity. All levels of existence need to be honored and kept in balance.

In conclusion, Neptune represents the sea of collective or universal feelings and emotions. He is considered the unconscious collective. Through him, we dissolve our personal egos and merge into the deep

---

43 Hand, Pg. 206

realm of the emotions. Through him, we experience spiritual cleansing and are able to attain a state of bliss or ecstasy.

Key Words for Neptune

Abstract, acceptance, aesthetic qualities, aesthetic, artistic, assuming, beauty, bliss, chanting, chaotic, chemicals, clairvoyance, compassion, compulsions, confined, confusion, connection with poison, counterfeit, covert, creative inspiration, creative, dance, deception, deluded, denial, dependence, devotion, dishonest, dissolution of forms, divinity, doubtful, dreams, dreamy, drug and alcohol abuse, ecstasy, elusive, emotional, empathy, escape, essential, euphoric, exceptional, fanciful, fascinating, formlessness, fraud, fraudulent, generosity, gift for harmony and rhythm, gullible, hallucinations, hidden, hypnotism, hysterical, idealism, idealistic, ideas, illusion, illusions of perfection, imagination, impressionable, inclusive, indulgent, insanity, insidious, insight, inspiration, inspired, intuition, irrational, joy, lack of commitment and direction. liquids, loss of life direction, love, Maya, mediumship, memories of past, morbid, musical, mysterious, mystic, mystical perception, naïve, nebulous, neurotic, Nirvana , non-attachment, obscure, ocean, overly imaginative, past, peace, penetrating, places of seclusion i.e. jails, asylum, poetic, poor mental health, pretense, prophetic, psychic abilities, receptive, receptivity, romantic, sacrifice, sarcasm, self-deception, self-destruction, self-sacrifice, sensitive, separateness, serenity, service, silence, solvent, spiritual undertaking, subconscious mind, subliminal, subtle, sympathetic, tranquil, transformation, transpersonal, ultimate reality, universal love, universal oneness, unreality, unreliable, utopian, vague, victim, visionary, water, withdrawal.

Key Concepts for Neptune

On an inter-psychic level, Neptune dissolves our defense mechanisms, allowing unconscious material to surface. He erodes our sense of personal individuality; his influence disintegrates and separates us from our more peripheral traits. Neptune represents our desire to return to the womb, to our spiritual Source or to God. He is our desire to return to Eden, our existential longing to return home. This planet represents the process of sacrifice and surrendering to the Universal Self.

Neptune blurs the line between the finite and infinite, between the material and spiritual realms of existence. He is a unifying agent, one who dissolves the barriers between the conscious, personal unconscious and collective unconscious. In our quest for spiritual enlightenment, there are also dangers, especially of losing all touch with material reality.

Pluto

> *"Through Pluto we are capable of penetrating to the very core of all existence. Through her, we are able to delve into our personal unconscious in order to surface suppressed or repressed material".*

Pluto enables us to face our own demons, especially those unacceptable parts of our psyche that deal with power and control. Her energy eliminates the outworn, creating change both on individual and social levels. On the individual level, she represents the dissent into the very core of our being. The procedure is much like Dante's journey into Hell, which is a symbolic excavation, confrontation, acknowledgment and finally acceptance of all of characteristics. Pluto penetrates through our evil, as it were, in order to get to the other side where we are made complete and whole.

> *"The journey into Hell symbolizes the descent into the unconscious, or the awareness of all the potentialities of being cosmic and psychological-that are needed in order to reach the Paradisiac heights,*

except, that is, the divine chosen few who attained to these heights by the path of innocence". [45]

An important component of this decent is confronting the image of the negative feminine force or the Medusa, which in psychological terminology is the interjected "terrible mother". She is an image of death; the cruel side of man which is indifferent to human suffering. This mother figure is devouring; she both gives life and can take it away. She is that part of the experience with our mother that was disappointing, that let us down and instilled in us a large measure of shame. She is identified with any negative traits that occurred in the early environment. This is especially true of any dubious characteristics in the primary caretaker that could not be acknowledged by the child because of his dependency on that individual for his survival. Any negative qualities of the mother figure are adopted by the child and in a sense, take on a life of its own. The process involves segregating the caretaker figure into two or more parts. The parental figure retains the beneficial attributes while the destructive and inept segments are internalized and repressed. We are capable of internalizing early disappointments resulting from our needs not being met. The abusive effects can continue even into adulthood masquerading as jealousy, lust, envy, or a desire for omnipotent power and control.

Pluto is the energy or power source, which compels all life to constantly renew itself and adapt to change. Her power is intense, unceasing and relentless. She is our highly focused internal desire to both surface and eliminate obstacles to positive development.

The strength or force of Pluto is proportional to the difficult task she must accomplish. This is why she is traditionally associated with possessing tremendous power. However, if her might is perverted through

---

45: Cirlot, Pg. 165

misuse and personal gain, it results in a variety of very negative consequences: obsessions, compulsions, paranoia, and projection. In this specific situation, projection means placing the blame or abdicating the
responsibility for one's own power to someone else. We can misuse our
power to manipulate others, either directly or indirectly.

In essence, she is the very heart of change itself. As the concept of
thanatoes was equated with the sign Scorpio, Shiva, an East Indian god,
can be associated with Pluto. She is a god of contradictions: to keep the
world in balance, she must destroy to sustain life. She brings death and
destruction but also joy and re birth, wisdom and peace. She, like Pluto
embraces both the terrible and benign. Pluto is also a paradox in that it
must destroy in order to make room for new life. It is the agent of death
and decay but also rebirth and renewal. It can be associated with both
the process and actual products of decay such as waste materials.
However, this "waste" becomes the very energy source that regenerates
life. Her regenerative properties extend into the realms of sexuality. It
represents sexual passion, the instinctive biological urge to procreate
and the phase that is reproduction itself (as opposed the sex act).

In conclusion, she is considered the lord of the underworld. Pluto is
the principal of beginnings, endings, death, re-birth, and change in general. She is the longing to undergo a symbolic death and to be born
anew. Pluto intense energy is played out in the arena of relationships
and sexuality. Through the act of sexual union, we experience a type of
death of our individual separateness. She drives us on towards self-
transformation and is the impulse towards growth. Pluto is the continual cycle of destruction and re-building of life.

Key Words for Pluto

Able to delve into one's deepest psychic levels, able to transform,
agent for change, breakdown, compulsions, controlling, courage, crav-
ing, cruel, death, deep, depth, desire to understand motivation behind

experiences, eliminate, evolving, explosive, endurance, initiation, intense, intrigue, intuition, lust for power, manipulate, obsession, parts of sexual expression, power hungry, power, probing, reformulation, renewal, resourceful, resurrection, ruthless, sadistic, secrecy, self-centered, strength, will, willful, willpower.

Key Concepts for Pluto

Pluto penetrates to the very core of existence. We are able to summon the courage to face our own demons or unacceptable facets of our psyche. This is especially true with issues revolving around power and control. Her energy both eliminates and transmutes that which is antiquated. Pluto allows change both for the individual and society.

Pluto can represent any internalized negative qualities of the mother figure from childhood. The internalization first involves segregating the caretaker figure into two or more parts. The parental figure retains the benevolent attributes while the destructive or inept traits are internalized and repressed by the child. Negative qualities of the mother are embraced by the child and, in a sense, take on a life of their own.

Pluto is the energy or power source that compels all living things to constantly renew and adapt to change as needed. Because Pluto's power is so intense, unceasing and relentless, change is inevitable. The experience of pain is also part of the Plutoneon process of renewal. We experience mourning the loss of an old image of ourselves.

The experience of pain is also part of the Plutoneon process of transformation and reorganization. Pain is engendered as we discard false attachments, identities, or belief systems in order to embrace new ones. We experience mourning the loss of an old image of ourselves. Change inherently engenders feelings of loss, the surrendering of prized parts of us; this inevitably can results in grief, sadness and guilt.

Chapter Seven

Houses

Each dimension of existence or planet is met and lived out most intensely in the area or House of the chart in which that planet resides. It is the "where" factor in the astrological equation.

The horoscope is divided into twelve houses, which make up the 24-hour period during which the earth rotates once on its axis. There are four major points to the chart.

Left side or Eastern Hemisphere

Ascendant: Is the sign, which was emerging over the eastern horizon at the moment of birth. The sign is the key to the relationship between the individual and the environment, a door or gateway though which the individual looks out at the world and through which the world looks back. It is a two way process: how we see the world conditions the experiences we have which in turn reshapes our viewpoint of the world. It is our persona or public image. Persona is related to the word person and personality, which comes from the Latin word for mask. When we are out in the world, it is the mask we put on for others. In a sense it can be considered the good impression we hope to present to society.

Right side or Western Hemisphere

Descendent: It is the sign on the cups of the 7th house of marriage, and signifies those qualities, which we are seeking in a partner. However in reality they are those attitudes which are unconscious within us and which need to be discovered and reclaimed in order for us to have a well balanced perspective on life. The key idea is to integrate all of our attributes.

Upper half or Southern Hemisphere

Midheaven, MC or Medium Coeli: It is the sign on the cusp of the tenth house, which suggest our relationship to the visible parent. It mirrors faucets of that parent's nature which are more responded to by the child. Also, it is the way we would like to be seen by that parent and by society at large. They are qualities we try to work towards, social values received from that person, lessons to be learned in life, and obstacles to be made conscious and integrated into our personality. They are also qualities inherited from that parent that we want to develop for ourselves. It is how we want to be viewed by society. It is also engaging in those types of activity that makes us happy especially in the context of our careers.

Lower half or Northern Hemisphere

Imum Coeli or Immum Coeli: The qualities of the sign on the cusp of the 4th house are deeply submerged and unconscious. They are at the very root or source of our basic nature. They are the very core meaning of who we are that tends to be hidden from others and ourselves. It is the symbol of the parent that was least visible to the child.

First House

> *"The first house and Aries bring the basic feeling "I exist", the desire to emerge into life with conquest, self-assertion and initiative; the "I am", the inner sense of beingness and primary identity also belong to this house. The physical appearance is said to be described by the Ascendant..."* [46]

The first house represents beginnings: it is the initial step in the process of becoming a whole or complete individual. It represents the mind-set we carry with us, the fashion or manner by which we start anything new. It is associated with our energy level and our physical appearance. It is the how we appear to others, rather than what we actually look like. In the context of the first house, our body is the instrument by which we initiate movement and action in the world. If that ability is hindered, it can result in various forms of disease. Our body is our identity in motion.

Through developing the sign of the ascendant and utilizing planets in the first house, we become aware of ourselves as individuals. Because the first house is in opposition to the seventh (one on one relationships), we develop a unique sense of being a separate person or "I", as we interact with another individual or "you".

In conclusion, first house and specifically the Ascendant is much like an aperture or lens through which energy both enters and exits, it is our chief point of inter-connection with the environment. We have a symbiotic relationship with our surroundings; energy is transmitted to us and visa versa.

46: Reinhart, Pg. 100

Key Words for the First House

Aperture, appearances, beginnings, character, energy level, initiation, outer appearance, persona, personality, self-interests, sense of "I" in here.

Key Concepts for the First House

The 1st house represents beginnings: it is the initial step in becoming a whole or complete individual. It is associated with our energy level and the appearance of our physical body, which is our identity in motion.

Second House

> "The proper use of possessions leads to the revelation, exteriorization, and fulfillment, in relation to other human beings and to one's society, of one's individuality, that is, who one is. A person realizes what he is by using what he owns; he demonstrates what he is to himself and all men, by what he was given at birth along with what he constituted acquire later on. Ideally, he should transform these possessions in terms of his individual purpose and destiny". [47]

The second house is where we develop the concept of what we value, like to gain and acquire in life. It represents what we desire to possess; the kinds of inherent faculties, resources, and capabilities we have or can develop. By utilizing our talents and through our possessions, we experience a sense of substance, value, greater self-worth, safety and security. This house represents our attitudes in general towards the material world and how we approach earning money and developing

---

47: Rudhyar, Pg. 64

skills. It is our psychological mind-set of what we find valuable. Valuing is an identification of who we are with what we value; in that sense what we find valuable indicates the type of person we are.

In conclusion, through this house, we connect with something external and identify it as part of us. This process of attaching and identifying who we are with external objects is the inherent meaning of the second house. It also indicates how we use the possessions we own. It is the part of our ego structure that is willing to go beyond the boundaries of the physical body and attach itself to external objects, making them a part of us. It is where we seek to enhance our sense of security through accumulating objects of wealth. It makes resources both internally and externally available in our lives.

Key Words for the Second House

Financial affairs, internal and external resources, money prospects, security, skills, talents, and valuables.

Key Concepts for the Second House

The 2nd. House is where we develop our image of what we value, like to gain and acquire in life. Through utilizing our talents and through our possessions, we experience a sense of substance, value, greater self-worth, safety and security. This process of attaching ourselves to and creating an individual identity based upon the objects that we possess is the inherent meaning of the Second House.

Third House

> *"The third house is involved in left brain activity, our mental style*
> *or how we think, and our attitudes towards learning in general; it is*
> *where we learned how to apply logic and reason."*

It exemplifies the exchange of information through all forms of communication. It deals with our rational and sequential thought patterns, the logical and analytical part of our brain. It initiates us intuitively into the world of symbols and language. Here is where we develop our ability to speak, to express ourselves verbally. The third house is the place we develop our specific style of compartmentalizing and classifying data. The third house describes what we contribute to the immediate environment as well as what we take from it. We perceive and select certain features of the environment while filtering out others. It is the assemblage of a code of practical rules and truths, which gives order and meaning to our lives.

It is our experience of early education. It is responsible for certain conditioned responses and the formation of habits based on repetition of behaviors. These activities are performed without having to consciously think about them. The fourth house portrays early emotional conditioning, while the third represents our early mental and psychological conditioning and describes the intellectual atmosphere in which we were raised. This area of the chart signifies the patterns of thought or mental scripts we developed in our early environment and for the most part carry with us into adulthood.

It is our pre-conscious mind, that level of brain activity, which operates just below conscious awareness; it is our reactive mind. In other words, this house symbolizes the automatic responses we make in everyday life: it is our "auto-pilot" (Robert Hand's term).

In conclusion, it is our conditioned responses or habits learned through repetitious behavior. These automatic responses can represent such simple activities as riding a bike or playing a musical instrument or more complicate ones such as our attitudes to life. House three stands for the conscious learning of mental and physical functions through repetition, which in turn makes theses behaviors, operate automatically. It is also referred to as the house of short journeys because it is here where we explore our immediate surroundings. This house also symbolizes close relatives such as siblings, aunts and uncles, neighbors and all matter of behaviors established with close relations. In essence, it entails relationships and activities, which operate on a spontaneous and familiar level with a minimum of conscious effort.

Key words for the Third House

Aunts and uncles, communication, lower mind, neighbors, routine short trip, siblings.

Key Concepts for the Third House

The 3rd. represents our pre-conscious mind, that level of brain activity which, for the most part, operates just below conscious awareness. It is our reactive mind.

It is our conditioned response to varying situations and habits learned through repetitious behavior. The 3rd house exemplifies those parts of the mind responsible for conscious learning of mental and physical functions through repetition. This repetitive procedure of learning then makes these responses operate automatically. This house also represents close relatives such as siblings, aunts and uncles, neighbors and all matter of behavior established with close relations.

Fourth House

"On the most fundamental level, the fourth house represents the sense of me-in-here: it is the integration of a variety of information around a central figure or "I" which forms the basis of our identity".

The fourth is where we sustain a stable and consistent portrait or concept of ourselves. It is the most private self and the root source of our being from which we operate to meet life. It is the psychic function that connects us to the rest of life. It allows us to feel that we belong, and are at home within ourselves: here, we are connected with all of existence.

Fourth house matters include whatever supports our physical and emotional well being. In terms of resources, it provides the actual materials needed for us to survive.

It represents our family of origin, close relatives and others with whom we have a parental like relationship and experience support and nurturing. The tenth-fourth houses is the parental axis in the natal chart. The fourth represents the hidden parent of either gender. It is the one who remained on the sidelines, who was clandestine, a mystery to the child. It should be noted that the image of one's parents is highly subjective; the way they are perceived by the child may not actually represent who they truly are. Children, through their own unique filtering process will create a benign image of this fourth house figure to insure their survival.

The fourth house also represents our immediate community, our primordial ties with past generations; it includes our relationship to family legacies and memories inherent from our ancestors and the human race in general. In essence, this house signifies any locale where we feel comfortable enough to relax and call home

In conclusion, on the deepest level, it is the storehouse of emotional and psychological patterns or constructs genetically imputed or formulate through the conditioning or scripting we received in our early environment. This includes infantile and pre-natal experiences. These early impressions are stored in the deepest, unconscious emotional levels and may surface in adulthood as habits and emotionally based behavioral patterns whose origins are unknown. Our experience with our family is the earliest influence upon which we built a relationship to society in general. This house represents how we operate within social settings. And finally the fourth house represents endings, specifically around how we resolved and deal with closure in our lives.

Key Words for the Fourth House

Ancestors, closure, community, endings, habits, hidden parent, me-in-here, private self, root, sense of belonging, support.

Key Concepts for the Fourth House

Fourth house matters entail whatever supports our physical and emotional well being. The 4th-10th houses are the parental axis. The 4th. represents the hidden parent of either gender. Children, through there own unique filtering process will create the image of this 4th. house figure based on the sign on the IC and planets associated with that area of the chart. This house represents how we operate within social settings. And finally, the 4th house represents endings, specifically how we resolved and handle closure in our lives.

Fifth House

> *"A rather self-involved influence, the fifth house affords us through our creative expressions, a sense of identity and the ability to fulfill our need to be someone special, influential and loved."*

In the fifth, we play out our desire to be recognized for some unique quality, especially some form of artistic endeavor that truly represents who we are. In essence, it is where our will to create can materialize. It also shows the style and manner in which we create and through this act, enhance our self-worth. Here we are able to experience total immersion into what we are doing, become fully engaged and absorbed into our activity. Here we are offered the opportunity to surrender our ego to the collective creative source.

The fifth house represents any action or activity in general that makes us feels good: it is where we can both give and receive pleasure from others and our surroundings. They are activities that are done just for the sake of doing. It is anything that can be considered play and which we carry out merely because it is what we want, like and choose to do. It is important to remember that fifth house activities are those we select to engage or participate in and are not executed out of necessity.

In conclusion, the sign on the cusp plus any planets situated in or are involved with this house describe the type of person we choose as the object of our affections. Usually they are relationships formed simply for social and sexual pleasure. The enjoyment experienced with another in a light, carefree manner typifies fifth house activities. It is the house of love affairs but not of marriage. Further, incorporating both the creative and sexual symbolism encountered in the fifth, it exemplifies the creation of children as extensions of who we are and as a form of self-expression. And finally, the fifth is the house of our symbolic inner child, that part of us that wishes to play, to be spontaneous, noticed, natural, special and innocent.

Key Words for the Fifth House

Artistic expression, childbearing, children, create, creativity, gambling, love affairs, places of amusement, pleasurable emotions, self-expression, and speculation.

Key Concepts for the Fifth House

In the 5th house, we desire to be recognized for some form of creative expression or artistic endeavor that represents who we truly are. It is important to remember that 5th house activities are those we choose to engage or participate in and are not performed out of necessity. Enjoyable experiences with others in a light, carefree manner typifies 5th. house activities. It is the house of love affairs but not of marriage. Further, incorporating both the creative and sexual symbolism encountered in the 5th, we create offspring as an extension of who we are and as a way of expressing ourselves.

Sixth House

"In the sixth house we develop discrimination, and begin defining ourselves by what we are not; we begin thinking reflectively and desire self-improvement; we develop skills and the perseverance to apply them". [49]

The sixth house defines our natural boundaries and our need for self-definition. We encounter experiences, which help us to learn humility, accept our human limitations and take responsibility for our own state of psychological and physical health.

Here is where we learn to serve a purpose or function specific to our inherent nature. Through the rigors of this house, we become or evolve into what we are meant to be. It is here where we take stock or inventory of ourselves and choose our priorities in life. Here, we are accountable for how we are utilizing talents and capacities. The focus of this house is recognizing our limits through experiences that are usually considered humbling. Specifically, we learn about our bodies need to set limitations through the experience of ill health. Illness is a symptom of negative energies, which are difficult for the mind and body to handle. Illness is the representation of underlying psychological problems manifested on the physical plane. It involves factors that interfere with the bodies functioning, factors in the inner or outer life of an individual that are being denied expression. Illness is the consequence we must endure if we do not respect our shortcomings. It is the manifestation of

---

49: Reinhart, Pg. 132

disease or dis-order that warns us that something is wrong. It is a flag, which signals our need to explore the mind-body or psyche-soma connection, that relationship between the inner world of mind and feelings with the outer world of body and form. When we respect our limitations, we then remain within the parameters of good health. The sixth house, in essence, asks us to bring our mind, body and emotions into harmony. It offers us a place to refine, perfect and purify ourselves.

The sixth is the house of our relationship to work. It pertains to self-denial and postponing self-gratification. Sixth house activities are those pursued not for their own sake (as in the fifth) but to provide service to others. It is the house of employers and employees; it represents our attitudes towards daily, mundane tasks, which we find is necessary to perform in order to assure our survival. It is not our vocation or career, but activities which sustain us on a day to day basis. Our career or vocation falls in the tenth house.

In conclusion, it is involved with dispensing authority over others and in turn, how we handle being in the subservient role. Relationships that are formed out of necessity, duty or responsibility rather than out of pleasure or for the sake of expressing ourselves fall in this house. It symbolizes how we feel in general about being of service to others, the way we manage our time and how we function with everyday tasks and life's necessities.

Key Words for the Sixth House

Day-to-day tasks, deferred gratification, duty, employees, hygiene, illness, mind-body connection, necessity, servants, service, sickness, subservient, work or job,

Key Concepts for the Sixth House

Specifically, in the 6th house, we learn about our bodies' needs and limitations through the experience of ill health. It involves factors that interfere with the bodies functioning, factors in the inner or outer life of an individual that are being denied expression. The 6th house, in essence, asks us to bring our mind, body and emotions into harmony. This is the house of day to day responsibilities. It deals with self-denial and postponing self-gratification. Sixth house activities are those pursued not for their own sake (as in the 5th house) but for the sake of providing service for others

Seventh House

The Descendent is the sign on cusp of the seventh Houses of marriage, representing those qualities that we seek in a partner yet in reality are unconscious traits within us that need to be re-discovered. The key idea here is the integration of all of our attributes.

The first house and ascendant initiates the process of self-awareness, while the seventh and descendant refer more specifically to becoming aware of others, especially on a one to one level. In the seventh, we begin developing relationships with others.

The seventh deals with our approach to relationships and the qualities we seek in a partner, it is also the house of marriage and open enemies. It represents two individuals joining together, each one is the others reference point. In effect, each partner functions as a mirror reflecting back to the other key characteristics and traits of that person. It is where two individuals joined together for a mired of reasons, these include creating a family, gaining security, stability and lessening loneliness. The sign on and any planets in this house, describes the type of partner we are searching for, plus the conditions under which the relationship will form and what that union will be based on.

In conclusion, because the seventh also represents those individuals who are in competition with us, it is also referred to as the house of open enemies. In a deeper sense, open enemies refer to unacceptable attributes that we project onto others. These displaced negative qualities make the other person seem like our enemy. We may not like a certain person because he reflects traits that we do not wish to accept within ourselves. It is referred to as the house of the inner partner (Liz Greene's term) because here we are really attempting to unite ourselves with these projected attributes. The seventh house represents relationships in which there is intimate contact between the subject and "I" and the object or "you".

Key Words for the Seventh House

Awareness of others, competition, intimacy, marriage, open enemies, partner, partnership, and relationships.

Key Concepts for the Seventh House

The 7th deals with our approach to one on one relationships, and the qualities we seek in a partner; it is also the house of marriage and open enemies because it represents those individuals who are in competition with us. In conclusion, the 7th house symbolizes relationships in which there is intimate contact between the subject and "I" and the object or "you".

Eighth House

> "In Scorpio and eighth house we seek personal justification, to overcoming our separateness and become more than ourselves; we grow through our deep encounters with others and our desire to be at one with them. Here we find the powerful themes of sexuality, birth, death, loss and abandonment, emotional destructiveness, rebirth and regeneration". [50]

50: Ibid. Pg. 145

The 8th house represents other people's values and possessions, psychic and occult matters, inheritance including emotional, psychological patterns and physical disabilities and the type of careers, which involve other people's money. It describes the manner in which we interact with another on a very deep and intimate emotional level; this theme of merging underscores the sexual dynamics of this house. It can also signify our abuse of power over others as a way of making us feel secure.

The 8th also has to do with a couple's resources, collective needs and value system. It is the house of sex, death and regeneration. It represents certain aspects of sexual union, especially the experience of the orgasm. The eight exemplifies the loss or letting go of our ego-boundaries when we are involved intimately with another.

We experience a type of death when we unite with others on a very deep and emotional level. Two individuals together form a more inclusive third entity, in which the whole is greater than the sum of its part. They are the types of relationships in which our partner can bring out the very best or worst characteristics in us. Through intimate bonding, or giving of ourselves to another completely, we descend into the essence of our true being. As unresolved issues surface from our past, we are given here the opportunity to both cleanse and rejuvenate ourselves. Problems encountered in this area usually involved repressed anger, jealousy, and desire for power and control based on early childhood necessities and the relationship with our initial caretakers. The ultimate goal is to both admit and accept these emotions and learn to channel and contain their explosive potential. Experiences in adult relationships tend to parallel those encountered in early childhood. These situations afford us the opportunity to understand the connection between our present relationships and those problems encountered with our caretakers early in life. The 8th house provides us with self-knowledge and mastery. We are helped to recognize, accept and transform the beast within, those dark sides of our personality.

This house stimulates an interest in what is hidden and mysterious in life. It familiarizes us with death and the process of dying through exposing us to situations involving change. It is house of transformation through death (either literally or figuratively), resurrection and renewal through our intimate relations.

In conclusion, this house exemplifies those experiences that represent our inner drive for change, and in particular intimate relationships, which bring them about. It is all exterior events and circumstances that stand for transition. All situations that involve breakdown, decay and rebirth are represented by the 8th. It also includes any circumstances in which we are forced to relinquish our possessions. It is where we experience a subconscious inner drive toward growth and transition. It also involves removing anything that hinders our self-improvement.

Key Words for the Eight House

Career dealing with other's finances, collective value system, death, inheritance, intimacy, mystery, occult, others values and possessions, psychic, rebirth, sexual union, transformation.

Key Concepts for the Eight House

The 8th is the house of sex, death and regeneration. We experience a type of death when we unite on a very deep and emotional level with another. Experiences in adult relationships tend to parallel those encountered in early childhood. The 8th house provides us with the gift of self-knowledge and mastery.

This house represents experiences that reflect our inner drive towards change; in particular, they are alterations in our lives that intimate relationships we are involve in, bring about. The 8th house is where we experience a subconscious inner drive mobilizing us towards growth and change.

Ninth House

"The ninth house is where we both consciously observe and attempt to understand the underlying patterns in our environment. It is the perspective we get when standing back and observing life at a distance".

It is the energy, which allows us to explore the world. The chief goal here is seeking truth through developing philosophical systems and religious beliefs in order to understand the underlying patterns and basic laws governing life. This process helps us find purpose and meaning in life, to discover the Absolute from which we form ideals and goals to aspire to. We learn through searching for and participating in activities which widen our horizons and expand our consciousness: what we learn here, helps us to create a more uniform identity. We are able to establish a personal philosophy or belief system, through which we can better understand the world around us. It symbolizes both a journey of the mind and actual long physical journeys where we find ourselves in unfamiliar circumstances or situations, which are out of our usual day-to-day routine. This house also describes the manner in which we pursue religious and philosophical issues; it also includes how we develop our concept of the Divine or God.

The ninth is the house of the higher mind and the seat of right brain activity. It is where we convert and synthesis incoming data into patterns or concepts we can understand. The ninth house is the area of our chart where the symbol making capacity resides. This particular tool helps us to see life in a Gestalt or holistic manner. The ninth house help us to learn about relationships, specifically those that help us to understand how all things are interrelated and integrated with one another through a common underlying pattern of energy. It is also concerned with our interaction with the external world. In essence, the ninth house helps us to understand that we are truly part of all life. We are able to derive meaning from our experiences because we inherently understand that behind all isolated events, there is an overall pattern to life and that we are indeed part of that mosaic.

In conclusion, on a more mundane level, the ninth house embraces higher education and institutions of learning. It relates to foreign countries or anything that may seem remote from our normal existence; this includes different philosophies and religious or cultural traditions from our own. Through our ability to organize data into meaningful systems and because of our collective impulse to attain the ideal, the ninth also represents legal systems and bodies of law, especially the higher courts. It can also indicate what field of study we might choose in college. Basically, the ninth is a vehicle through which new ideas, modes of thinking and new perceptions are made available to us.

Key Words for the Ninth House

Philosophical, concept of God, concept formation, pattern recognition, integration, long journeys, higher education, institutions of learning, legal system, religion, religious belief, grand overview of life.

Key Concepts for the Ninth House

The 9th house is where we both consciously observe and attempt to understand the underlying patterns in our environment. This aptitude helps us to grasp and understand life in a Gestalt or holistic fashion. It is here we understand how all things are interrelated and integrated with one another through a common underlying pattern of energy. On a more mundane level, the 9th house embraces higher education and institutions of learning. As an extension of this house's capacity to organize data into meaningful systems, and because of its systemic drive to attain the ideal, on the collective level, the 9th also represents legal systems and bodies of law.

Tenth House

> *"In the 10th. House the individual meets experiences that result from the fact he has succeeded, or failed, in gaining a social position that is, a place in the complex ritual of social, public, or professional activities. He is integrated, or fails to become integrated, into the greater whole in which he has learned, or failed to learn, to participate cooperatively. He has a place, a definite function, a public status in his own community".* [51]

The sign and any planets associated with the tenth house and the Midheaven symbolize those characteristics that are most visible to the general public; they are traits that stand out the most. The 10th is where we develop that particular part of our identity involved in social interaction. It is the way we behave when we are out in public, the image we present to the world: it is the individual out in the world performing a social role. The sign and planets associated with this house also indicate those qualities for which we are admired, respected and looked up to by others. The 10th is the way through which we hope to achieve honor and recognition, status and prestige. These accomplishments are what we would most want to be remembered as having contributed to society.

This house represents a process of evolution, something that we are trying to become, a role in this life that we aspire but have yet not attained. The 10th signifies our social status, honor and reputation. The nature of our personal best expressed in a social setting; it is where we attempt to put our best foot forward. It represents the nature of our contributions, status and place in the world. It is our reputation, position in the world and our true vocation and career. This is in contrast to the sixth house where the work that we do is out of necessity and which

---

51: Rudhyar, Pg. 117

we might not especially enjoy doing. It also signifies the type of career we are involved in and more importantly, it signifies the approach we have towards fulfilling our career ambitions. It is here where we derive a sense of identity from participating in our occupation, and in general from what we do or are involved with in a social context. A person may not get his identity from his career, but instead, this may, come about through vocational activities, which the general public recognizes him for.

It is a symbol of the highest conscious level to which we may aspire: it is where the various energies within us come together in the most perfect manner. As part of the 4th/10th parental access, the 10th represents early bonding patterns we had with the parent who was most visible to us; it was whoever was responsible for teaching us the rules and protocol of society and who disciplined the family. It was the parent who was most supportive of our efforts, and who motivated us. The 10th is the parent who supplied us with key information to help us grow and sustain ourselves in the world. The characteristics of the sign and planets associated with the 10th house describe the dominant parent, but more importantly it represents this internalized parental figure. It can also indicate those characteristics of that parent, which were never expressed but are now lived out through the child. The relationship between the child and that particular figure, influences how we relate to authority figures in adulthood. Again, its position is not relegated to only the biological male or father figure, but to anyone who played that particular socializing role.

In conclusion, the tenth is the house of relationships with authority figures in general: it is our experience of those who act as disciplinarians, those with power over us including bosses, employers and government officials. In the general sense, the 10th represents unequal relationships in which one party plays the dominant role while the other, the passive one. In the dominant position, the other individual can serve the specific function such as teacher, guide, role model or mentor. If matters are reversed, we can also serve in that capacity. In this context, we are the student to the master or one who is knowledgeable in a particular discipline.

Key Words for the Tenth House

Achievement, activities, ambitious, authority figures, bosses, business, disciplinarians, dominant-passive, employers, evaluation, fame, parenting, government officials, guide figures, honor, inequality, most visible, profession, promotion, recognition, standing in the community, status, substance, super-ego, vocation.

Key Concepts for the Tenth House

The sign on the Midheaven and any planets in the 10th house symbolize those characteristics of an individual that are most visible to the general public. The 10th is where we develop our sense of personal identity through participation in society. It depicts our social status, honor, reputation and the nature of our contributions, status and place in the world.

As part of the 4th/10th parental access, the 10th represents early bonding with the parent who was most visible to us. The characteristics of the sign and planets associated with this house describe this dominant parent, the now internalized parental figure that had the most authority over us. The relationship with that particular individual influences how we relate to authority figures as an adult. In a general sense, the 10th represents unequal relationships with another in which one party plays out the dominant role while the other, the passive one.

Eleventh House

"Syntropy—the tendency life-energy to move towards greater asso-
ciation, communication, cooperation and awareness—is the main
principle upon which the eleventh house operates. Having recog-
nized ourselves as separate and distinct individuals there is the call
to reconnect with everything from which we have previously differ-
entiated ourselves". [52]

The 11th house is where we attempt to go beyond our ego-identity and become something greater than what we already are. It is where we strive to identify with something larger than ourselves; it represents our overall relationship to society and is an expression of who we are in social situations.

Through the eleventh house we are able to integrate our personal identity with that of the groups: it represents relationships which deal with one person relating to many. This house also includes friendships or any relationship in general that are casual. It also signifies how we go about making friends and our behavior with them. Friendships expand both our boundaries and resources.

In essence, this house portends our ability to get along in any situation in which we have to relate to several people at once, and where we have to modify our behavior to get along. This house is where we can expand ourselves, establish contact with others and become integrated into a group. It deals with shared group ideals and aspirations plus our ability to identify with other people and make the identity of the group a part of us.

52: Sasportus, Pg. 94

This feat requires balancing or harmonizing our personal needs with those of the group and society as a whole. Through group affiliation, we are able to enhance our feelings of security and fulfill our need for social and intellectual camaraderie. It is where we can associate with others who share similar ideas and objectives. Here, we strive to find security in the knowledge that there are others of like mind. We are able to include, as part of our self-identity, membership in something that is greater than just us alone.

It is here, where we connect with all of life, and hopefully realize that we are a part of a greater whole, and are interconnected with all of creation. We transcend the boundaries of our individual existence to experience ourselves as part of the larger community of mankind. The eleventh represents the tendency of all of us to gravitate towards greater association, communication, cooperation, and awareness. As individuals, we participate in and serve the function and progress of the group; we promote the purpose and reason for its existence. This, however, requires us to relinquish some of our personal urges, needs and desires for the sake of the collective.

In conclusion, the eleventh house represents social consciousness. It is where we are able to experience a connection with all like-minded people. We are able to discover our relationship to the whole of the human race. It is here, where we strive to implement needed humanitarian and political changes. It also characterizes the type of group we are attracted to and the style in which we interact in-group settings.

Key Words for the Eleventh House

Aspirations, friendships, goals, group membership, group relationships, humanitarian interests, life's desires, our hopes and wishes, shared group ideals, situations we have no control over, social consciousness, social groups.

Key Concepts for the Eleventh House

The 11th house is where we identify with something larger than ourselves; it represents our relationship to society and the integration of our personal identity with that of the organization. It represents relationships, which deal with one person relating to many. This includes any type of relationship that is more superficial then intimate such as memberships in social groups. It deals with shared group ideals and aspirations. It is our ability to identify with other people and make the identity of the group a part of us. It also characterizes the type of group we are attracted to and the style in which we interact in-group settings. It is the house of friendships, i.e. those particular types of relationships that expand our boundaries and resources.

Twelfth House

> *"The twelfth house is where we take our first fledgling steps into the world, the first expenditure of our energy into the environment".*

However, this may or may not be received well by those around us. If we are rebuffed for some reason, that energy (represented by the sign on and any planets in the twelfth house) is withdrawn and becomes hidden away in our sub-conscious. These experiences may involve events or emotional traumas while still in the mothers' womb up to the first year of our life.

The mother can convey her fears and apprehensions to the unborn fetus. We may repress our reaction to this negative energy and express it later through chronic illness. We may also project this dynamism outward and on to others. Those traits we fear in ourselves are acted out through individuals in our environment; in time, we may begin to feel victimized by them. The twelfth house represents our desires and urges, which we may not be consciously aware of. They are characteristics that we hide from ourselves and which may eventually seem like our enemy. Those suppressed dimensions of ours can work to sabotage our goals and objectives in life.

There is a general theme of dissolution in the twelfth. Here is where we experience releasing our egos and merging with something greater. It is where we desire to transcend personal limitations, separation and fulfill our systemic longing for union with the infinite.

This house represents what Carl Jung termed the "collective unconscious" or the precursor and foundation of our individual psyche. However, as inviting as this may be, it is met with an equally strong counter force. It is our dread of non-being, of loosing our individual self. Our desire to transcend the ego can manifest through more benign channels as medication, devotion, prayer and selfless service to others. It can also be acted out through less wholesome venues as drug and alcohol abuse and even insanity.

Through devotion and selfless service to others, we develop empathy and compassion, important positive characteristics associated with this house. The service we perform for others may actually help us to heal our own 12th. house difficulties.

The 12th house requires us to surrender our need to control our life and learn to accept whatever may come along, to have faith and keep strong even during times of sorrow and difficulty.

In conclusion, this is the point in our chart where we can tap into the creative power of the collective. From this source, we can draw upon the collective muse for inspiration. It is here where we find great wisdom and inner treasures that lie waiting for us to unearth and benefit from in our lives.

Key Words for the Twelve House

Betrayal, collective unconscious, confinement, creativity, illusive, devotion, disappointment, dreams, exile, fancy, fantasy, health, hospitals, illusion, imagination, limitation, losses, places of retreat, redemption, romance, seclusion, secret enemies, self-undoing, self-sacrifice, service, sorrow, transcends, transformation, visions.

Key Concepts for the Twelfth House

The 12th house represents those desires and urges that we may not be aware of and as such can work to sabotage our goals and objectives in life. We may repress those characteristics and experience them in the form of chronic illnesses.

This house represents what Carl Jung termed the "collective unconscious" or the precursor and foundation of our individual psyche. Through devotion and selfless service to others, we may develop empathy and compassion. They are important and positive traits we may improve upon through this house. The services we perform for others may actually help us to heal our own 12th house difficulties.

END

Bibliography

Ansken, Ruth Nanda, The Mystery of Consciousness; A Prescription for Human Survival, (Moyer Bell)

Bergson, Henry, An Introduction to Metaphysics, (New York, NY Bobbs-Merril), 1955

Burr, H. F., The Fields of Life, (NewYork, Ballantine, 1972)

Campbell, Joseph, The Hero with a Thousand Faces, (Princeton University Press, 1949)

Carter, Charles, E.O., The Principles of Astrology (Wheaton, Ill, A quest Book, The Theosophical Publishing House, 1963)

Cirlot, J.E., A Dictionary of Symbols, (Dorset Press, 1991)

Devore, Nicholas, Encyclopedia of Astrology (New York NY. Philosophical Library, 1947)

Fritjof Capra, The Tao of Physics (New York: Balitime, 1977),

Goldbery, Philip, The Intuitive Edge, (Boston, Mass., Horghton Muffin Co.)

Greene Liz, Saturn: A New Look at an Old Devil, (Samuel Weiser, Inc., New York NY) 1976

Greene, Liz, Relating, An Astrological Guide to Living with Others on a Small Planet (York Beach, Maine: Samuel Weiser, 1978)

Hamaker-Zondag, Karen, Psychological Astrology: A Synthesis of Jungian Psychology and Astrology. (York Beach, Main Samuel Weiser, Inc., 1989)

Hand, Robert, Horoscope Symbols (Rockport, Mass., Para Research, 1981)

Levi, Grant, Astrology for the Millions, (St. Paul, Minn. Llewellyn,) 1973

Lundsted, Betty, Astrological Insights into Personality (San Diego, San Diego Astro Computing Services, 1980)

Microsoft, Encarta Encyclopedia 99 1993-1998 Microsoft Corp.

Oxford Book of Psychotherapy

Perry, Glen, Birth of Psychological Astrology (Article on the Internet)

Reinhart, Melanie, Chiron and the Healing Journey: An Astrological and Psychological Perspective (London England, Arkana, Penguin Books, 1989)

Roberts, Herbert A., The Principles and Art of Cure by Homeopathy, Quote from: Organon of the Healing Art; Hahnemann, Vide Oragaon 43 (Devone, England, Health Science Press, 1979)

Rudhyar, Dane, The Astrological Houses: The Spectrum of Individual Experience, (Doubleday Paperback, Garden City, NY) 1972

Sasportus, Howard, The Twelve Houses, An Introduction to the houses in astrological interpretation, (Wellingborough, Northamptonshire) 1985

Vithoulkas, George, The Science of Homeopathy, (New York, NY. Grove Press, Inc. 1980)

About the Author

Vic Purcell holds a master's degree in Educational Psychology. He has extensive experience in the field of human resources, has been a psychological counselor and currently is an astrological practitioner in private practice. He has also taught courses in psychology astrology and has written numerous articles on this subject. In essence, he bring to the honored position of astrological practitioner, a unique blending of both traditional academic training in psychology combined with extensive knowledge of the most up to date principles of humanistic oriented astrology. He can be reached at VicPurcell@netscape.net